POLICY AND PRACTICE IN ⎯⎯ ꜱꜱᴀᴌ ꞔAꞦE
NUMBER TWENTY

Asset-Based Approaches:
Their rise, role and reality

POLICY AND PRACTICE IN HEALTH AND SOCIAL CARE

See www.dunedinacademicpress.co.uk for details of all our publications

POLICY AND PRACTICE IN HEALTH AND SOCIAL CARE
SERIES EDITORS
CHARLOTTE CLARKE AND CHARLOTTE PEARSON

Asset-Based Approaches:
Their rise, role and reality

Fiona Garven
Director, Scottish Community Development Centre

Jennifer McLean
Public Health Programme Manager, Glasgow Centre for Population Health

and
Lisa Pattoni
Head of Innovation and Improvement, Institute for Research and Innovation in Social Services

EDINBURGH ◆ LONDON

First published in 2016 by Dunedin Academic Press Ltd.
Head Office: Hudson House, 8 Albany Street, Edinburgh EH1 3QB
London Office: 352 Cromwell Tower, Barbican, London EC2Y 8NB

ISBNs:
978–1–78046–052–9 (Paperback)
978–1–78046–557–9 (ePub)
978–1–78046–558–6 (Kindle)

Shelfie

A **bundled** eBook edition is available
with the purchase of this print book.

CLEARLY PRINT YOUR NAME ABOVE IN UPPER CASE

Instructions to claim your eBook edition:
1. Download the Shelfie app for Android or iOS
2. Write your name in **UPPER CASE** above
3. Add your book in the Shelfie app
4. Download your eBook to any device

British Library Cataloguing in Publication Data
A catalogue record for this book is available from the British Library

Typeset by Makar Publishing Production
Printed in Great Britain by CPI Antony Rowe

CONTENTS

ACKNOWLEDGEMENTS

The authors are pleased for the opportunity to write this book, which seeks to bring together three differing perspectives on an area of mutual and growing national interest. We would like to thank Series Editor Charlotte Pearson for her guidance in the development of the text. We would also like to thank the organisations and colleagues of the Institute for Research and Innovation in Social Services (IRISS), the Glasgow Centre for Population Health (GCPH) and the Scottish Community Development Centre (SCDC) for their ongoing support, encouragement and interest in our work.

We would like to extend our thanks to a number of people who shared their views, insights and experiences with us, and who helped to inform and contribute to our thinking, in particular: Akwugo Emejulu, Alison Petch, Angela Morgan, Angus Wood, Carol Tannahill, Catherine Rose Stocks-Rankin, Cathy Sharp, Clare Black, Doreen Grove, Eric Duncan, Frances McBride, Francesca Lynch, Gehan MacLeod, Harry Burns, Janet Muir, Karen McCulloch, Lauren Johnston, Nick Wilding, Olivia Hanley, Paul Morin and Rory MacLeod.

We would also like to thank our families and friends for their support and patience during the development and preparation of *Asset-Based Approaches: Their rise, role and reality*.

This book brought together a new working partnership and friendship for the three authors, which over the course of many (many) conversations has resulted in a greater awareness of each other's area of work and a more rounded understanding of the successes, implications and challenges to asset-based working across interconnected disciplines. Finally, in the development of this book, we have been privileged to spend time with and hear the stories and experience of many people, from a range of different backgrounds and perspectives, all of which continue to be a source of inspiration.

GLOSSARY OF ABBREVIATIONS

ABCD	Asset-Based Community Development
AI	Appreciative Inquiry
CA	Contribution Analysis
CDAS	Community Development Alliance Scotland
CHEX	Community Health Exchange
CHIP	Children's Inclusion Partnership
CLD	Community Learning and Development
CLDMS	Community Learning and Development Managers Scotland
CoSLA	Convention of Scottish Local Authorities
GCPH	Glasgow Centre for Population Health
GDP	Gross Domestic Product
GPI	Genuine Progress Indicator
HDI	Human Development Index
HELP	Health Empowerment Leverage Project
HLC	Healthy Living Centre
IRISS	Institute for Research and Innovation in Social Services
ISEW	Index of Sustainable Economic Welfare
IWI	Inclusive Wealth Index
LEAP	Learning, Evaluation and Planning
MBCT	Mindfulness-Based Cognitive Therapy
NEF	New Economics Foundation
NGO	Non-governmental organisation
PAGES	Parent's Advisory Group for Education and Socialisation
PB	Participatory Budgeting
PDSA	Plan Do Study Act
RCT	Randomised Control Trial
SCDC	Scottish Community Development Centre
SCN	Scottish Co-Production Network
SPRU	Social Policy Research Unit

ToC	Theory of Change
UNEP	United Nations Environment Programme
UNUIHDP	United Nations University International Human Dimensions Programme
WARM	Well-being And Resilience Measure
WHO	World Health Organization
WRAP	Wellness Recovery Action Planning

AUTHOR BIOGRAPHIES

Fiona Garven is Director of the Scottish Community Development Centre (SCDC), which incorporates the Community Health Exchange (CHEX) and the Scottish Co-Production Network (SCN). She is the Chair of Community Development Alliance Scotland (CDAS), a trustee of Irvine Housing Association and a non-executive director of North Ayrshire Women's Aid. Fiona has specialist expertise in community development. Her main areas of focus are community engagement, building community capacity and community-led approaches to health. She has a background in community learning and development (CLD) and has many years' experience of implementing community development approaches across several sectors. Fiona's current work includes action research into asset-based approaches, support for community-led regeneration, democratic renewal and policy advice on community development approaches to public service reform. Her main interest lies in evidencing and profiling the benefits of community development methodology in order to create strong, healthy and equal communities.

Dr **Jennifer McLean** is a public health programme manager at the Glasgow Centre for Population Health (GCPH), where she co-leads a research programme exploring asset-based approaches and resilience for public health, with strong interest in the theory and evidence base underpinning the approach and asset-based working in community and healthcare settings. Jennifer is also the lead manager for the pSoBid study, which explores the social, biological and psychological determinants of ill health in Glasgow, and also contributes to GoWell, a study of housing, health and regeneration in the city. Prior to taking up this post Jennifer worked at NHS Health Scotland in a national research management role and with NHS Ayrshire and Arran as a public health research officer following the completion of her academic career. She is also an honorary lecturer at the University of Glasgow.

Lisa Pattoni is the Head of Innovation and Improvement at IRISS (Institute for Research and Innovation in Social Services). She has a wide range of interests around collaborative and co-produced methods of working and at IRISS her work involves supporting people to learn and reflect together, take risks and improve outcomes through the adoption or adaptation of new approaches. Lisa also currently serves on the Children's Panel, which is a role she finds challenging and rewarding in equal measure. Her work often crosses the boundaries between academia, policy and practice, and prior to working at IRISS Lisa held and enjoyed roles in or influencing all these areas, mainly from within the not-for-profit sector. Communicating and interpreting ideas, policy and research have always been at the heart of her work.

INTRODUCTION

Inequality in Scotland continues to grow (Leyland *et al.*, 2007; Thomas *et al.*, 2010; Beeston *et al.*, 2013). If we are to achieve a fair and just society with positive outcomes for all, there is an imperative to examine both the structural causes of poverty and inequality and the role that public services play in mitigating and reducing their impacts.

It could be argued that a model of public service delivery based on a 'deficit approach' has evolved – focusing on problems, needs and deficiencies of individuals and communities, designing services to fill the gaps and fix the problems. This leads to individuals and communities becoming both disempowered and dependent. In effect, we continue to generate demand rather than address the root cause of health and social inequality. For politicians, policymakers, practitioners and citizens, it is clear that more of the same will not do. Examining current issues through the lens of an asset-based approach allows us to think differently about the relationship between the state and the citizen, and the service provider and people using services.

This book aims to provide a critical overview of the evidence for asset-based approaches, including background and rationale for the approach, the current policy, political and economic context, and the implications and opportunities for the workforce (health, social services and community development). Particular attention has been paid to the developing debate in Scotland, with lessons and learning drawn from work undertaken nationally.

In recent years discussions about asset-based approaches have started to permeate several areas of public policy in Scotland. The debate originated in the context of public health, largely stimulated by the interest of the (then) chief medical officer (CMO), Sir Harry Burns, whose research recognised the changing nature of disease in society and the importance of well-being and individuals feeling in control of their lives and their social circumstances. He highlighted that, although life expectancy is increasing for the population as a whole, the big public health issues of today (alcohol and alcohol-related violence, suicide, obesity) continue to be a cause of unacceptable ill health, which is inequitably distributed across society. It was therefore proposed that it may be time to change the methods we currently use to improve health and to move to more asset-based approaches to enhance outcomes, focusing on what keeps us healthy, rather than what makes us ill.

Since the publication of the CMO's annual reports on public health in Scotland in 2009 and 2010 (Scottish Government, 2010a; 2011a) and the seminal report of the Christie Commission (Christie, 2011), which underlined the need to focus on prevention, the debate has expanded across several areas of public policy, most notably the broad area of public service reform. Asset-based approaches are now being seen as an important lens through which to examine and develop the changing relationship between the citizen and the state and between those supported by services and those doing the supporting. This has implications for emerging policy in Scotland and the structures and cultures of public services. Arguably, strength and capacity can be built through agencies working together with individuals and communities as equal partners. Changing demographics, resource constraints, increased demand, rising patient and public expectations, and the changing nature and burden of disease have led to increased interest in the role of individuals and communities in tackling health and social inequalities and in improving well-being.

However, despite this growing interest and increasing numbers of people engaging with the debate, a number of central questions remain. How meaningful is the terminology of asset-based approaches within the context of the recession and austerity? How far is it realistic to expect individuals and communities to absorb the gaps that are left by potential reductions in state services? How can we support a workforce tasked with simultaneously maintaining essential services at the same time as being asked to embrace the challenge of new ways of working and thinking? Is there sufficient appetite and capacity within individuals and communities to engage with this agenda? We will consider and discuss these questions in *Asset-Based Approaches: Their rise, role and reality.*

Throughout this book we argue that a focus on 'assets' does not negate the value and need to address structural circumstances that lead to poverty and inequality (such as distribution of wealth, access to employment and education, and social inclusion) in order to improve quality of life for individuals and communities. Rather, the approach brings into sharper focus the need to redress the balance between deficit-based approaches and asset-based working to enhance the well-being of individuals, families and communities.

As the debate is not confined to one specific policy area, this book considers asset-based approaches from three broad perspectives: those of public health; community development; and social services. We make the case that the fundamental values and principles underpinning asset-based approaches are common to all three areas of work and that they all share ambitions concerned with improving health and well-being, reducing the inequality gap and improving life circumstances for all. Despite this, language across all three areas remains inconsistent; there is a lack of a common evidence base and a lack of coherence across policy and practice operating at the individual, community and population level. The scale of the literature and evidence base available related to each of these perspectives is diverse and we have not therefore been able to go into depth in relation to all themes of interest explored. We have tried instead to ensure that we have considered the broad contexts for public health, social services and community development to draw out the shared challenges, opportunities and common factors associated with asset-based policy, thinking and practice. This text has given us the opportunity to examine some of these issues through drawing on our own knowledge and experience and those of others, to help expand and contribute to the debate. We hope it will be of interest to those from a policy and practice background alike.

Our approach

Asset-based approaches are primarily about people. In this spirit we have written this text by drawing on the people within our networks, who have been positive assets in the development of the book. Our first step was to arrange a small informal session with practitioners from across health, social services and community development to draw on their experience and wisdom to help inform us about what they would find helpful in a resource about asset-based approaches and some of the important themes we should consider within the text.

Our interview approach

Building on this spirit of participation, our second step was to conduct a series of informant interviews with ten people to draw out the experiences, insights and voices of people using asset-based principles in practice. These interviews enabled us to capture the stories, lived realities and perspectives of a range of people. Interviewees were drawn from national and local perspectives across health, social care and the community and voluntary sector (see Figure 0.1).

Interviewee number	Interviewee's profession/background
1	policymaker
2	health practitioner
3	community-based project manager
4	academic
5	community development manager
6	community development manager
7	academic
8	non-governmental organisation (NGO) manager
9	NGO practitioner
10	academic and advocacy practitioner

Figure 0.1: Professions and backgrounds of individuals interviewed to provide a wide practice perspective.

Interviews were carried out in a location convenient to the interviewee and they lasted forty-five minutes to an hour. Informed consent was sought prior to each meeting, which was conducted within a fairly open framework. This allowed for focused, conversational, two-way communication, providing not just the answers to the questions asked but also the opportunity to discuss reasons for the answers. Key areas of interest discussed with all interviewees included: how they would describe an asset-based approach; why this way of working was appropriate from their perspective, and what was different about it; the outcomes achieved for people and places; the strengths and barriers and constraints of this way of working in projects and service; and what needs to change or happen to ensure that asset-based approaches underpin practice.

Quotes from these interviews are used throughout this text in order to bring the evidence base alive and to provide further context to illustrate key points from practice. Although these quotes are not personally attributed, we provide an indication of the person's experience in relation to the topic to help the reader understand the perspective that is being represented.

The use of case studies

Throughout the text we also include a series of case studies to give further illustrations of asset-based working in practice. These relate to the focus of each chapter, across a range of different projects, services and settings. They are intended to demonstrate practical experiences of adopting and embedding asset-based principles across a range of settings that are addressing complex social issues in a more holistic and innovative manner than has traditionally been taken. Case studies used in the book are listed in Figure 0.2. Two of them have been sourced and adapted from the literature as cited (see Figures 3.1 and 6.1); all other cases have approved their inclusion within this text.

Case study figure number	Title
2.2	Children's Inclusion Partnership (CHIP), North Glasgow
3.1	Wellness Recovery Action Planning (WRAP)
3.4	GalGael Trust
3.5	Parent's Advisory Group for Education and Socialisation (PAGES)
4.1	Talking points
5.2	Includem
6.1	The Buurtzorg approach

Figure 0.2: Illustrative case studies used in *Asset-Based Approaches: Their rise, role and reality.*

Structure of the book: An overview

Asset-Based Approaches is presented in three main sections, with two chapters within each section, focusing on the rise, role and reality of asset-based approaches respectively, in a Scottish context.

Part 1: The rise of asset-based approaches

In Chapter 1 we outline the context for the assets debate, centring on issues of inequality and social justice. We examine the previous policy landscape that has led us to where we are today, from community development, social services and health perspectives. Within this chapter we look at current aspects of policy and legislation that support asset-based approaches and discuss the role of democracy in shifting the relationship between the state and citizens.

In Chapter 2 we pose the question 'what is in a name?' and focus on the language of asset-based approaches. We discuss whether asset-based approaches are reinventing or revitalising an existing concept. What do 'assets' and 'asset-based approaches' actually mean? What are the values and principles that underpin this way of working? Finally we address the question 'Spot the difference: Asset-based approaches, community development or strengths-based approaches?'

Part 2: The role of asset-based approaches

In Chapter 3 we consider 'what difference do asset-based approaches make?'. We give an overview of the outcomes that we can expect to see through the implementation of asset-based approaches at individual, group and community, and population level, and offer some practical examples of what asset-based approaches look like in practice.

In Chapter 4 we focus on the nature of evidence, by discussing and examining how asset-based approaches help us to reconsider 'what we measure', 'how we measure' and 'what counts as useful evidence'. We then discuss the challenge of evaluating asset-based approaches and draw on some available tools and techniques to assist the measurement of asset-based approaches at individual, group and population levels.

Part 3: The reality of asset-based approaches

In Chapter 5 we consider the kinds of enabling conditions and foundations that are required for asset-based approaches to develop, grow and thrive.

In Chapter 6 we examine the structural, cultural and behavioural challenges that contribute to the gap between the policy aspiration of asset-based approaches and the realities of practice.

Finally, we offer personal reflections on the key points raised in each of the chapters.

PART 1

The Rise of Asset-Based Approaches

CHAPTER 1

Setting the Scene: Asset-based approaches, why now?

Introduction

The debate about the benefits, constraints and appropriateness of asset-based approaches is currently taking place mainly within the context of tackling health and social inequalities, community empowerment, public services reform and democratic renewal. In Scotland, the attention of politicians and policymakers is turning increasingly towards the use of asset-based thinking and approaches in their attempts to respond to reductions in public spending, welfare changes, growing inequalities and an ageing population. In the midst of all this, academics and social commentators are providing analysis and critique both of the approach and the policy drivers, while managers and practitioners seek to make sense of implications for the adoption of the asset-based approach for their practice and the broader organisational systems and structures they operate within. Somewhat paradoxically, it could be argued that the people and communities, whose outcomes asset-based approaches are intended to improve, are furthest away from policy development and their voices are often least heard at the local level (Audit Scotland, 2014).

The role of government in setting policy for social issues is inherently complex. Policy development does not usually take place in distinct stages; it is often determined by events, and the effects of policy can be indirect, diffuse and take time to appear (Hallsworth *et al.*, 2011). Nonetheless, when thinking about the rise in profile of the current discussion and critique of asset-based approaches, it is important to reflect on past policy (and what we might learn from it), alongside examining the current drivers for the debate – in this case, in Scotland in particular.

This chapter sets out the context for the debate about asset-based approaches in relation to inequality. It briefly reviews past policy in relation to asset-based ways of working and describes the recent legislative and policy directives that support asset-based approaches in Scotland. The chapter concludes with commentary on how asset-based approaches link to new debates on participatory democracy, with a particular focus on the Scottish context.

The context of inequality

In the UK, and in many parts of the Western world and Latin America, the past few decades have seen an aggressive pursuit of neoliberal ideas based on free enterprise, the privatisation of public utilities enforcing a 'profit' imperative over norms of public service, and reductions in welfare and social services. In the UK the primary focus on economic growth has been supported by policies that have included tax incentives for big business and the deregulation of the labour market. At the same time the provision of welfare has been replaced by the notion of individual responsibility (Rustin, 2010). The mantra from successive UK government and governments across Europe and the USA has been that the trickle-down effects (Resolution Foundation, 2015) of economic efficiency and sustainability will benefit everyone in society. From the 1980s onwards, however, growth rates started to fall and unemployment rates rose, with the net effect of a reduction in consumer demand, increasing debt and the global collapse of the financial market.

As a result health and social inequalities across most of the developed world have deepened. Scotland is now the fourth most unequal of the OECD countries in terms of income inequality (Equality Trust, 2015), and the differences in life expectancy, depending on where you live, are stark. One example in a recent study showed that a man living in the East End of Glasgow had a life expectancy fourteen years less than his counterpart living only seven miles away in a more affluent part of the city (McCartney, 2011) (see Figure 1.1). In a similar study carried out in Edinburgh, evidence showed that a man living in Bankhead is likely to live nearly eleven years less than his counterpart in another, more affluent part of the city, only two miles away (ScotPHO, 2010).

There have been other effects of a neoliberal agenda and the reduction in state services. Arguably, a model of privatisation intended to bring more choice and improve quality has reduced the role of the state in ensuring a social responsibility for those who are most marginalised in our society and most dependent

Figure 1.1: Life expectancy for males in Glasgow (McCartney, 2011).

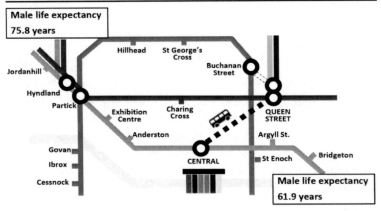

on state support, as providers are pushed to cut costs and deliver contracts more efficiently. Added to this there is evidence to suggest that, in the high-profile service areas such as education, health and neighbourhood planning, the most confident, well-networked and skilled citizens are better able to access what they need and to negotiate better outcomes for themselves and their families, further compounding inequalities across the population (Hastings and Matthews, 2011).

Across the UK we are witnessing a polarisation between the rich and the poor – the richest 1% of the population has as much wealth as the poorest 55% of the population combined (Inequality Briefing, 2014). It is now well documented that high levels of inequality manifest in increased adult and infant mortality, obesity, poor physical health and poor mental health (Wilkinson and Picket, 2009). Moreover this has a knock-on effect in the rise of social problems such as disenfranchisement and alienation, increased violence and crime, and it may also be a causal factor in civil unrest (Latchford, 2011).

The impact of this on the financial sustainability of our public services cannot be underestimated. Current policy discussions in the UK and in Scotland are increasingly focusing on thinking differently about how we deliver state services in ways that help tackle the effects of inequality on health and social outcomes and that move beyond a transactional relationship between service provider and service user (Christie, 2011).

Policy rhetoric and debate on public services reform in Scotland are increasingly concerned with reducing negative outcomes and adopting preventative approaches, with an emphasis on building services round individuals and communities. Democratic renewal is high on the agenda, signalling an overt move from government to governance, with government institutions encouraged to adopt an enabling role and work with others to release new resources for change (Taylor, 2003). At the level of community this means creating a new relationship between the state and the citizen through devolved decision-making and a reinvigoration of local democracy designed to empower local communities to have greater influence on state actions and to take action for themselves. In the context of the individual this translates as changing the relationship between professional staff delivering services and the people supported by services, by encouraging involvement in certain aspects of service delivery.

Learning from policy past

The involvement of people in public services is now prominent in current thinking and the benefits of community-led provision are becoming better understood. There is evidence that, over the past few decades, some aspects of Scottish legislation and social policy have already been moving in a direction that increasingly recognises the benefits that can be accrued – for government and citizens alike – in involving people in the issues that affect them. As far back as the Social Work (Scotland) Act 1968 and the duty therein to 'promote social welfare', the accompanying Scottish Office guidance stated that this would involve:

> the development of conditions whether for individuals, for families or for larger groups which will enable them to deal with difficulties as they arise through their own resources or with the help of the resources of their own community (as cited in Barr et al., 1995).

Nearly fifty years on, this guidance statement is not dissimilar to the current description of an asset-based approach to public services. In the context of the debate about asset-based approaches it should be recognised that some social movements such as the disability rights movement and recovery movement, among others, have always had the principles of involvement, self-determination and empowerment at their core. Famously, in the 1990s, the disability movement adopted the slogan 'nothing about us without us' to communicate the idea that no policy should be decided without the full and direct participation of the people affected (Campbell and Oliver, 1996). At the same time, and in the preceding decades, many disability rights organisations were formed explicitly to support the collective, representative voice of disabled people in promoting equality, human rights and social justice. One of the most notable Scottish examples of this has been the Glasgow Disability Alliance, established in 2001 and now with more than 3,000 members, which promotes the message:

> Disability is not about impairments or medical conditions – it is a complex social problem which requires joined up working across a range of agencies and the whole of society to remove barriers. In this way, disability shifts from being a private trouble and is identified as a public, social issue – a problem that has to do with the way society is organised rather than with individual deficit (Glasgow Disability Alliance, 2012).

Community development context

Community development, also with the values of empowerment and democratic participation at its core, emerged as a specific occupation in the UK in the 1960s, based on the idea that disadvantage and social injustice cannot be tackled by top-down solutions alone.

In 1966 the Gulbenkian Foundation set up study groups to examine the nature and future of community work in the UK. The Gulbenkian Report (Calouste Gulbenkian Foundation, 1968) characterised community development as:

- helping local people to decide, plan and take action to meet their own needs with the help of available outside resources;
- helping local services to become more effective, usable and accessible to those whose needs they are trying to meet;
- taking account of the interrelation between different services in planning for people;

- forecasting necessary adaptations to meet new social needs in constantly changing circumstances.

In response to the recognition that poverty was a major feature of British society, and to the debates on the value of the participation of citizens and local communities in various aspects of government activity – mainly local planning (Skeffington, 1969) – the Community Development Projects programme was launched in 1969. It was the largest action-research project ever funded by government, the intention of which was to gather information about the impact of existing social policies and services and to encourage innovation and coordination. The projects had a strong and explicit research focus and an emphasis on social action 'as a means of creating more responsive local services and of encouraging self-help' (Loney, 1983).

From the 1970s until the 1990s, community development in Scotland was based on a radical social work model (Popple, 1995), which sought to address the structural causes of distress. Notably Strathclyde Regional Council recognised the role the community development worker could make as part of a wider public policy response to tackling poverty and deprivation. In 1995, as a foundation of its social strategy, there were 161 community development workers in the Strathclyde Council Region alone, reporting in excess of 1,000 separate pieces of work with local communities on issues to do with community care, housing, anti-poverty, children and families and public participation (Barr *et al.*, 1995). At that time the responsibility for a community development function at local authority level sat within the Department of Social Work. However, since the 1990s, we have seen a retrenchment in social work from a community approach to a risk management, protectionist model, and a consequent reduction in the numbers of community workers in the most challenging communities (Petts *et al.*, 2001; Kemshall, 2002). At the end of 2014 Glasgow City Council Department of Social Work lost its last remaining community development workers as part of its ongoing reorganisation and restructuring.

In Scotland, community development as practised by local authorities has now been largely subsumed into community learning and development (CLD), which was previously known as community education. Following the Alexander Report (HMSO, 1975), most local authorities in Scotland restructured their youth and community and adult education services into community education services. At that time there was widespread debate among many policymakers, academics and practitioners on what community education comprised, but one commonly agreed definition was that it is:

> a process designed to enrich the lives of individuals and groups by engaging with people living within a geographical area, or sharing a common interest, to develop voluntarily a range of learning, action and reflection opportunities, determined by their personal, social, economic and political needs (CeVe, 1990, p. 2).

Despite new statutory regulations on CLD (discussed in brief later in this chapter), this area of work has in turn experienced reductions in resourcing as local authorities have sought to make savings on reduced budgets. In a recent survey of the CLD workforce, the majority of responses from local authorities, which employ around two-thirds of the workforce, indicated a decline in staff numbers (Education Scotland, 2015).

Health context

Healthcare policy over the last few decades has developed and strengthened towards a current focus on prevention, partnership, workforce development and performance (Scottish Government, 2011b). The 1997 White Paper *Designed to Care – Renewing the NHS in Scotland* (Scottish Executive, 1997) put forward the government's vision for improving health for all in Scotland. This was developed further in *Towards a Healthier Scotland* (Scottish Executive, 1999). These papers recognised Scotland's ill health as a cause for serious concern, and proposed coordinating resources capable of influencing health to take action across a number of levels: to improve life circumstances; to enhance life styles; and to address particular health topics including coronary heart disease, teenage pregnancy, cancer, smoking and alcohol misuse, with the overarching aim of tackling health inequalities.

This focus was reinforced in *Improving Health in Scotland: The Challenge* (Scottish Executive, 2003). Citizenship responsibility for health became a key theme, and by 2005 the Kerr Report, *Building a Health Service Fit for the Future,* initiated this focus in the context of the changing nature of healthcare delivery, stating that 'the NHS in Scotland and the public must work hand in hand if we are to deliver a health service that is fit for the future' (Scottish Executive, 2005a, p. 5). The report made a number of recommendations including:

- services should be redesigned to meet local needs and expectations;
- the need to view the NHS as a service delivered predominately in local communities rather than hospitals;
- a focus on prevention and integration;
- developing options for change 'with' people, not 'for' them, engaging the public early to develop solutions rather than having people respond to predetermined plans conceived by professionals (Scottish Executive, 2005a).

Delivering for Health (Scottish Executive, 2005b) then set out practical terms and actions on how to turn this vision for the health service into reality. Building on this background, *Better Health, Better Care* (Scottish Government, 2007) set out the (new) government's programme to deliver a healthier Scotland by helping people to sustain and improve their health, especially in disadvantaged communities, thereby ensuring better, local and faster access to healthcare.

Social services context

In the last three decades there have been substantial changes within social services policy. As described earlier, the Social Work (Scotland) Act 1968 (Scottish Parliament, 1968), amended by a range of subsequent legislation, provided the core policy framework for social services. The eventual enactment of the National Health Service and Community Care Act 1990 was the 'beginning of a political movement to respond to economic, demographic and professional pressures about the welfare of its citizens within their own communities' (Mason *et al.*, 2006, p. 1).

Since then a review of social work services in Scotland, *Changing Lives* (Scottish Government, 2006), led to a series of ten recommendations, which were aimed at preparing and supporting social services to be fit for purpose in the twenty-first century, so they could continue to 'rise to the challenge of supporting and protecting vulnerable people and improving the well-being of people and communities' (Scottish Government, 2006, p. 3). For asset-based approaches, the following recommendations were particularly relevant. Social work services:

- would be designed and delivered around the needs of people who use the services, their carers and their communities;
- must build individual, family and community capacity to meet their own needs;
- must play a full and active part in a public sector wide approach to prevention and earlier intervention;
- must become an integral part of a whole public sector approach to supporting vulnerable people and promoting social well-being.

The intention behind this policy was welcome and aspirational; however there were many systems and processes that acted as a barrier to implementation.

Over the following ten years a wide range of developments led to reform and improvement across social services. These included policies such the introduction of self-directed support. In relation to asset-based approaches, the majority of the advancement in social services policy has largely been at the level of the individual, although crucially *Changing Lives* (Scottish Government, 2006, p. 38) highlighted that:

> Community social work has, in the past, been promoted as a discrete activity, conducted apart from mainstream social work practice. A new approach is now needed, which positions social work services at the heart of communities delivering a combination of individual and community based work alongside education, housing, health and police services.

Interestingly *A Shared Vision and Strategy* for Social Services in Scotland (Scottish Government, 2015) places less emphasis on 'social work' and instead takes a wider definition to ensure the strategy is more reflective of the social services workforce as a whole. This suggests advancement in the thinking outlined in *Changing Lives* (Scottish Government, 2006), bringing social work in closer alignment with 'all services provided by local authorities and to commissioned services provided by the voluntary and private sectors to meet the identified needs of the communities they serve' (Scottish Government, 2015, p. 10).

Are we at a tipping point in policy?

If viewed through an 'assets lens' it seems that we have some foundations from which to build. As discussed so far, these draw on social policy frameworks and initiatives from the 1960s onwards, the work and experience of social movements and aspects of community development, social work and public health practice disciplines, which already have many of the same features as asset-based approaches. These will be discussed in further detail in Chapter 2.

We are also much clearer now about what does not work. Early in 2011, a paper published by the Improvement Service in Scotland noted that 'a substantial amount of Scottish public spending (the National Community Planning Group suggested that this could be as high as 40 per cent) is driven by "failure demand" ' (Mair *et al.*, 2011, p. 4). In other words, demand was created by preventable negative outcomes in individual and community lives.

This is not the place to attempt a detailed analysis of the many policies and processes that have led to failure demand, but arguably the priority given to economic issues at the expense of social development, alongside the reprioritisation of social work services from preventative- and community-oriented functions to an individual, protective approach, have been contributory factors.

Current policy context

What seems to be unique about the developing policy context in Scotland is that the debates across different policy areas are simultaneously converging from previously disparate silos into a more coherent dialogue on systems-wide reform, with people and communities as its central focus.

In 2007 Scotland adopted a new model of government, working towards the single purpose of creating a more successful country, with opportunities for all of Scotland to flourish through increasing sustainable economic growth; it was based on an outcomes approach (Scottish Government, n.d.b). The model rested on:

> an ambitious conception of what is achievable through such a partnership between the public sector and civil society. It [the outcomes model] places strategic leadership and the facilitation of cooperation between organisations and sections of society at the heart of the role of central government, rather than a managerialist view of the relationship of central government to others (Elvidge, 2011, p. 4).

Following the spending review in 2007 and in support of Scotland's new approach to government, a national performance framework containing fifteen national level outcomes and indicators was developed. A concordat agreement was reached with local government via the Convention of Scottish Local Authorities (CoSLA), which set out the basis for devolved budgets and new financial commitments between central and local government, as well as new performance monitoring and accountability systems in the form of single outcome agreements for each of the thirty-two community planning partnerships in Scotland.

In 2011 the Christie Commission Report on the reform of public services in Scotland was published, which has since become a central policy driver. This was considered a landmark in that the commission called for a new culture of early intervention and prevention and stated that one of the four 'pillars' of renewing public services should be that 'reforms must aim to empower individuals and communities receiving public services by involving them in the design and delivery of the services they use' (Christie, 2011, p. 26). In responding to the recommendations of the commission, the Scottish Government committed to reforming public services in Scotland so that they build on the assets and potential of individuals, families and communities (Scottish Government, 2011c).

Before the publication of the Christie Report, Scotland's (then) CMO, Sir Harry Burns, had started to stimulate interest in asset-based approaches to health improvement and tackling health inequalities, by drawing on the work of Aaron Antonovsky, an Israeli–American sociologist whose work focused on the relationship between stress and health and well-being. Antonovsky (1987) proposed that the fundamentals of human well-being that underpin health lie in fulfilling personal relationships and in lives with a sense of coherence and purpose. (His work is discussed in further detail in Chapter 2.)

Sir Harry Burns proposed that services and budgets needed to focus on those at risk from the pre-natal stage onward, and to nurture and extend networks across vulnerable communities and groups, by building on and strengthening their assets and confidence, and thereby their resilience. In his annual report for 2009 (Scottish Government, 2010a) he highlighted examples of community-led health approaches to tackling health inequalities, pointing out that Healthy Living Centres (HLCs):

> try to make a difference because they take time, build trust and network, inspire ambition, give hope and help individuals to feel good about themselves, their families, neighbours and communities and do well as a result. Being positive and optimistic, sometimes in the face of major difficulties and challenges is how HLCs work with their communities (Scottish Government, 2010a, p. 12).

Following on from this, and his subsequent annual report *Assets for All*, much debate on the role of communities and the role of service users began to emerge and the importance of asset-based approaches is becoming common language across policy sectors (Scottish Government, 2011a).

Similarly, in 2011, the then Welsh Assembly published its strategic action plan for reducing health inequalities, where it included 'developing health assets in communities' as one of its seven action areas (Welsh Assembly Government, 2011). In England no similar priorities have been set at national level, but several influential publications have put forward a vision of positive health and well-being, as well as the case for enhancing assets and building strong communities (Department of Health, 2012; 2014; NICE, 2014).

More recently, in Scotland, there have been many references made to asset-based approaches from the highest levels of the civil service, leading to what has become known as the Scottish Approach to Government (further discussed in Chapter 3). In

2013, in his speech to the Scottish Leaders' Forum, Sir Peter Housden, the Permanent Secretary to the Scottish government from 2010 to 2015, reaffirmed the government's commitment to an open and engaging form of government that based its approach to policy on outcomes, thereby ensuring the focus of public spending and action built on the assets and potential of the individual, the family and the community, rather than being dictated by professional silos and organisational boundaries. He further underlined this commitment in an article to the *Civil Service Quarterly* in June 2014, stating:

> the ethos of co-production and an asset-based approach is ground-breaking work. It challenges traditional roles and assumptions. To achieve outcomes, not just activity and outputs, an organisation has to think, plan and act differently – about its resources, programmes, staff, management and governance and, crucially, how it works with others and with the communities it serves (Housden, 2014, p. 25).

Within the context of this agenda, one of the challenges has been to shift the emphasis in local government from a centrally driven service supply model to one that works in an enabling way, supporting and working alongside community organisations, local interest groups and the wider population to help stimulate more active participation in communities and in democratic processes.

Since the development of the national performance framework in 2007, several changes have taken place at policy and legislative level in Scotland. These responded not only to the outcomes approach but also to the effects of the economic recession and related austerity measures, to changing demographics, to emerging public health issues and to deepening inequalities. The major policy and legislative frameworks are outlined in brief below.

Legislation

Arguably the most notable legislative developments relating to asset-based approaches are the: Community Empowerment (Scotland) Act, which was passed in the Scottish Parliament on 17 June 2015 and which received royal assent on 24 July 2015; the

Public Bodies (Joint Working) (Scotland) Act 2014 (Scottish Parliament, 2013c); the Social Care (Self-Directed Support) (Scotland) Act 2013 (Scottish Parliament, 2013a); the Community Learning and Development (Scotland) Regulations 2013, which came into force on 1 September 2013; and the Land Reform Bill introduced on 22 June 2015 and passed by Scottish Parliament on 16 March 2016 (Scottish Parliament, 2015b). The following section sets out these legislative developments in more detail.

Community Empowerment (Scotland) Act 2015

This Act (Scottish Parliament, 2015a) gives communities greater access to buildings and land ownership or lease for wider community benefit. It puts the right of communities to have their voices heard on a legislative footing through the ability to raise a 'participation request' to be involved in an 'outcomes improvement process'. It also requires Scottish ministers to consult people representing communities when determining and reviewing the national outcomes. In an attempt to address equalities issues, the legislation requires each community planning partnership to:

> identify each geographic locality in their area where persons experience significantly poorer outcomes than are experienced by persons who reside in other localities in that area or significantly poorer outcomes than are experienced generally by persons who reside in Scotland (Scottish Parliament, 2015a, p. 7).

Each community planning partnership then to prepare and publish a plan for each such locality.

Public Bodies (Joint Working) (Scotland) Act 2014

Within the integration of health and social services agenda, the Public Bodies (Joint Working) (Scotland) Act 2014 has placed significant investment on supporting public agencies to move towards a co-production model (this is discussed in more detail in Chapter 4) with people supported by services and communities. This further supports the provision of personalised and flexible services, planned and delivered from the perspective of the person, with a focus on shifting care from acute services towards care provided at home or in the community. Integration of health and social services also places renewed emphasis on the importance of 'localities', in the recognition that they should be an integral part of the health and social care partnerships, which will be held to account for local priorities.

Social Care (Self-Directed Support) (Scotland) Act 2013

While recognising the need for support, the emphasis of the Social Care (Self-Directed Support) (Scotland) Act 2013 is that individuals are 'expert' in their own lives and that they have a range of assets and skills at their disposal to use to support themselves. Self-Directed Support places choice and control at the disposal of individuals to purchase support and services that meet each person's individual needs. It also draws on their strengths, giving them greater control over adapting their care to changes in their circumstances or condition, thereby enabling people to maintain personal independence and well-being through their connections to friends, family, colleagues and other networks. Central to the policy is ensuring that people and practitioners are involved at all stages of design and delivery of support, a focus that is set out to support a move away from a 'one size fits all' service culture towards more personalised care and support for those who need it.

Community Learning and Development (Scotland) Regulations 2013

These regulations (Scottish Parliament, 2013b) place a requirement on local authorities to involve individuals and groups in the development and assessment of local CLD plans. This duty sits alongside the strategic guidance for CLD, which provides a clear statement that the purpose of CLD is to empower people, individually and collectively, to make positive changes in their lives and in their communities. This is enabled through learning, with a focus on improved life chances for people of all ages, personal development and active citizenship, and through stronger, more resilient, supportive, influential and inclusive communities.

Land Reform Bill

The Land Reform Bill proposes powers for ministers to intervene where the scale of landownership or decisions of landowners are acting as a barrier to the sustainable development of communities. Once implemented the Land Reform (Scotland) Act will create a public register of those with a controlling interest in land, make provisions to force land sales if owners block economic development, set up a Land Commission, improve the right to roam, strengthen 'common good' land status and give more rights to tenant farmers. Proposals for secondary legislation under the new Act relating to the community right to buy abandoned, neglected or detrimental land (which was initially introduced by the Community Empowerment (Scotland) Act) are subject to consultation.

Policy frameworks

Alongside legislative developments in Scotland, a number of high-level policy drivers are increasingly placing priority on collaborative working, which enables people to exercise choice and exert greater control over the types of support they need for better health and well-being outcomes.

Within health, the major policy drivers are the NHS Scotland *Healthcare Quality Strategy* (Scottish Government, 2010b), in which the government has set out its strategic vision for achieving sustainable quality in the delivery of healthcare services across Scotland, and the *20:20 Vision* (Scottish Government, 2011b), which provides the strategic narrative and context for taking forward the implementation of the *Quality Strategy*. Both of those drivers aim to put people at the heart of NHS Scotland and are committed to providing high-quality healthcare.

Furthermore the *20:20 Vision* (Scottish Government, 2011b) has been developed in recognition of the vital role of the workforce. Embodied within the vision is a commitment to valuing and empowering the workforce and treating people well (Scottish Government, 2013). To further strengthen this policy and delivery landscape, in late 2014 Scottish ministers announced that a review of the public health function in Scotland was to be carried out, with a focus on investigating and determining how public health systems and functions contribute to improving health and well-being outcomes across the life-course, and in reducing health inequalities for the future (Scottish Government, n.d.a).

In the regeneration arena, national policy now recognises the importance of investment in social regeneration alongside economic and physical initiatives (GoWell, 2007; Egan *et al.*, 2014). The outcomes to be achieved through regeneration as stated in Scotland's *Achieving a Sustainable Future* are economically sustainable communities, physically sustainable communities and socially sustainable communities, which 'put communities first, effectively involving local residents in the regeneration process and empowering communities' (Scottish Government, 2011d, p. 42).

Policy into practice

Although the policy and legislative environment, in Scotland at least, has many drivers in place to support asset-based approaches, there remains a lack of correlation between policy ambitions at a national level and the allocation of resources and initiatives in place at a local level, which can potentially support the outcomes policy frameworks seek to achieve. Central to this is the issue of reducing public funds and the difficult decisions that are required to be made on simultaneously continuing to protect services for the most vulnerable people in our society while investing in different ways of working, which can potentially mitigate negative outcomes further down the line.

Furthermore some commentators assert that some legislative frameworks, such as the Community Empowerment (Scotland) Act 2015 and the Social Care (Self-Directed Support) (Scotland) Act 2013 may even exacerbate inequalities unless resources are put in place to support those least empowered to access and make use of the legislation (SCDC, 2014).

Critiques of asset-based approaches point to the dangers of using the language of such approaches in policy (alongside other language such as 'building social capital') to shift the responsibility of the state on to the citizen (MacLeod and Emejulu, 2014). They assert that the language points to a tendency to focus on local communities themselves as the source of their own problems, and in so doing to 'responsibilise' them for finding their own solutions

– thus letting others 'off the hook' (Collins and Feeney, 2014). This is discussed in more depth in Chapter 6.

It is clear from the evidence of past policy and from well-researched critique and analysis that, if asset-based approaches are to achieve the outcomes we hope for (discussed in Chapter 3), they cannot be separated from issues associated with poverty and social injustice. They must be deployed alongside and supported by progressive policy, which seeks to address the root causes of structural health and social inequalities, works to equalise the balance of power and wealth in our society, and which articulates and measures what we mean by 'progress' in different ways to the accumulation of wealth (discussed in more detail in Chapter 4).

Asset-based approaches and their relationship with a healthy democracy

A healthy, participatory democracy is a foundation-enabling condition for an asset-based approach. Although central government has a crucial role in setting a new strategic long-term 'vision' of how public services need to act and look different, their role should not be to micro-manage local provision and practice; rather it should concentrate on creating the best possible conditions for local providers – statutory, third sector and community-led – to innovate (Bunt and Harris, 2009). A state that is too directive risks failing to make best use of the existing individual and community strengths at a local level (Brotchie, 2013); on the other hand, one that simply leaves communities to 'get on with it' risks exacerbating inequalities. Therefore, in creating enabling conditions, a balance for government is required between setting strategic direction and facilitating the space for local self-determination.

It could be argued that the most exciting developments in moving towards change is led not by policy directives but instead determined by individuals and communities. The groundswell of local action around the independence referendum in Scotland in September 2014 led to a re-engagement of many people with the democratic process evidencing that, where there is a real prospect of change, people will mobilise and lend their voices and their efforts to making change happen.

Social media commentators on the referendum noted the correlation between the debates on equality and the differences in voting patterns between areas in Scotland experiencing poverty and between those populations living in more affluent areas (Sir Harry Burns, Twitter, September 2014). The four areas with 'yes' majorities – Dundee (57.3%), Glasgow (53.5%), West Dunbartonshire (54%) and North Lanarkshire (51.1%) – all include some of Scotland's most severe areas of poverty. Other areas with marginal 'no' votes were Inverclyde (50.1%), North Ayrshire (51%), Renfrewshire (52.8%) and East Ayrshire (52.8%), which have similar socioeconomic profiles. But, in the most affluent areas of Scotland, the 'no' margin of victory was widest. It was noted by one commentator that the 88% and 90% turnouts tended to be in areas where there was less social deprivation – areas where, it could be argued, people are well served by the current constitutional framework (Harvie, 2014).

However involvement in election processes is only one way for people to exercise their democratic rights and act for change. The challenge is to understand the assets better and the energy we have in Scotland for creating transformations both in the ways in which we run our democratic systems and for the kind of Scotland we want to live in. The question is perhaps not about how policy directs this but how public services can facilitate and enable space for people to get involved to direct adjustments from the ground up:

> Making Scotland a fairer, healthier and wealthier place will not be achieved without a democracy in which people can see how decisions are made, and where communities are active participants in that process (CoSLA, 2014, p. 14).

Scotland's governance is based largely on a system of representative democracy. Our democratic participation is centred on turning out to vote for the political parties that best represent our views, trusting that they will then implement policy to support the kinds of things we each want for our families, our communities and our country. Unless voters are actively involved in political parties, campaigning groups and organisations, or local action groups, our involvement in the democratic system is remote. Although recent turnouts in Scotland have increased, at a UK level over the years many people have disengaged. Since the 1950s, electoral turnout for national and local elections has fallen (House of Commons, 2013) as the distinctions between the political parties with a chance of gaining power have become blurred and our choices feel reduced.

In 2013 CoSLA set up a commission on strengthening local democracy in Scotland. In 2014, immediately prior to the independence referendum, the commission published its final report, which advocated the need to reinvigorate local democracy founded on the premise that 'it is fundamentally better for decisions about these aspirations [fair work, health, safety, sustainability, social services and education] to be made by those that are most affected by them' (CoSLA, 2014, p. 4). The report called for a move away from a centralist model, recognising that people are more likely to engage democratically when the decisions to be made are likely to affect them directly, and that only local democratic processes can engage with the diversity of local circumstances, needs and issues across Scotland's communities – especially in a time of reducing public finances.

But what has the issue of local democracy got to do with asset-based approaches? To support a move away from a central to a local system, CoSLA (2014) promotes the idea of participatory democracy working alongside traditional representative democracy. Participatory democracy can take many forms and can extend across formal processes such as participatory budgeting (see Chapter 6), and can also include supporting people to shift change through becoming active in community life and civil society. In the same way that asset-based approaches recognise the inherent strengths in all of us, a system of participatory democracy values the knowledge, understanding and experiences of local citizens and recognises those contributions as critical in shaping responses. A participatory system offers people the chance to become an active member of society, to play an integral part in how we shape and govern our communities and to contribute to a collective accountability and responsibility for how we manage and control the issues that affect our lives in an ever-changing world.

This approach correlates with the sense of coherence theory discussed in Chapter 2. If part of what makes us healthy is the ability to understand our own circumstances and exert some level of control over what happens in our lives then the ability to participate in local democratic processes offers a route through which we can make sense of our circumstances and take actions to influence the services we use and the systems that impact on our lives and the lives of our families and neighbours.

It could be argued that our reliance on a largely representative democratic system, often far removed from everyday life and the kinds of issues that directly affect us, has led to a lack of control ingrained in our culture, which in turn has contributed to a dependency on decisions and accountability for what happens to us to take place elsewhere. Leading academics on democracy suggest that current failures in public engagement stem from the kind of citizen that we are invited to be, which is typically spectator or complainer (Escobar, 2014).

Now we have an appetite for reinvigorating and reimagining our democracy, and a government that has stated its commitment to asset-based approaches and co-production, the questions for us now have to be focused on how change can take place, what this means for the public services and what this entails for communities.

Conclusion

Over last few decades, across many aspects of public policy, we have seen a progression towards citizen involvement and an understanding of the positive outcomes that can be associated with working with people in ways that support them to be 'part of the solution', rather than part of the problem. This idea is not new, and it is clear that there is much to be learnt from past policy, its successes and its failures, and also much to be gleaned from the work of social movements past and present, whose work sits firmly within a model that recognises the strengths and assets of the individual and the collective.

In Scotland, in particular, the policy environment is beginning to cohere around asset-based approaches as the core of the way in which we deliver public services, with the debate centred firmly within the context of economic, health and social inequalities. Also at the core of public services reform in Scotland is democratic renewal, supporting people to become more involved in community life and in the way we shape and deliver public services. But, although the policy environment in Scotland is increasingly embracing asset-based approaches, it could be argued that ingrained structural and cultural issues remain barriers to implementation. It is also clear that the wider social and political context of poverty and inequality cannot be ignored and that asset-based approaches will not, on their own, address the root causes of structural health and social inequalities.

In the next chapter we consider the range of definitions that are used to describe asset-based approaches. We discuss the theory base, the principles of the approach and its relationship to other forms of participatory practice.

CHAPTER 2

Defining Asset-Based Approaches

Introduction

In this chapter we focus on the 'language' of asset-based approaches. We describe what 'assets' and 'asset-based approaches' actually are and what this way of working means in practice. We also highlight current criticisms and challenges of the approach, and present the fundamental values and principles that underpin the approach. The chapter concludes by considering the key question of whether asset-based approaches are the same or different to community development and strengths-based approaches.

Throughout the chapter quotes are used from our interviewees to further illustrate and reinforce key points from a range of perspectives and from practice. A case study is also presented to demonstrate a current example of a project adopting and embedding asset-based principles for addressing complex social issues in a holistic manner across a whole community.

What's in a name?

An asset-based approach means different things to different people in different contexts. Even though it is defined and described in various ways, at the heart is the common thread of supporting people through recognising, valuing and building strengths, skills and talents, without disregarding the structural, social and economic challenges or circumstances an individual may be confronted with. The range of ways in which asset-based approaches can be described is illustrated in the quotes below from two of our interviewees:

> 'It's an approach that seeks to support people, discover their own strengths. But more than that discover their own ability to be self-determining.' [academic]

'It's an approach that acknowledges that we all have gifts to bring, that we all have something of value to contribute in a variety of settings, and it's really about <u>how</u> we work with that without sort of disregarding the challenges and the weaknesses and the structural inequalities that people also are confronted with.' [community-based project manager]

As discussed in detail in Chapter 1, the term is now permeating the work and function of the Scottish Government (Housden, 2014; Scottish Government, 2014) and is evident across a raft of different policy areas. The cross-cutting nature of the approach is further illustrated below:

'I think the asset-based approach is an appealing framework, or perspective, that's viewed as being widely applicable. And I think that's why it's been taken up by workers across a range of sectors.' [community development practitioner]

Policy commitment however only sets the imperative for change; the approach will be retained and embedded only if the benefits of it can be demonstrated in population health and economic terms (A. Morgan, 2014). There is however a movement towards a shared understanding of the terminology and more importantly a mutual agreement about the value and principles that underpin this way of working. At the heart of this is a 'person-centred' approach that insists that everyone is unique, and has a unique contribution to make to their organisation or community (O'Leary *et al.*, 2011) – an appreciative approach that recognises the intrinsic worth of people and places.

Reinventing or revitalising?

Nevertheless when apparent 'new ideas' come along, there is often confusion, misinterpretation and/or misunderstanding about the concept presented and the rationale behind it (A. Morgan, 2014). Although the term 'asset-based approaches' is new for some, for many others it is considered to be 'old wine in a new bottle' and 'is helping practitioners find new ways of tackling old issues' (O'Leary *et al.*, 2011, p. 6). As such, the discourse that has emerged over the last few years about the helpfulness of the language of assets and asset-based approaches suggests that it is:

- ○ community development with a new name;
- ○ naïve to think that we can live without needs-based or deficit approaches just by involving people;
- ○ overly focused on assets and thereby ignores or overlooks structural and material inequalities (Friedli, 2012a; A. Morgan, 2014).

The specifics of language are important in framing the ethos of the approach. This is particularly clear for asset-based approaches where the language of strengths and capabilities helps to steer the professional and the citizen away from the more traditional focus on needs and deficits (Brotchie, 2013). It can however also add a layer of opaqueness and ambiguity. Overcoming this issue is a major challenge for the approach, where good asset-based practice may be obscured by the use of other terminology. Similarly, practice may be called asset-based where it is not, in order to attract funding and fit with the current policy environment. There is also the danger of 'accepted wisdom' in relation to the use of asset-based language, where, although the term becomes part of the language and is cited in local and national policy, practice has not changed to reflect the language and underpinning premise of the approach.

The language used in community-led approaches and across systems and services, which aims to illustrate the way we work, can often be complex and, like that of asset-based approaches, can mean different things to different people and to different organisations. This point is further illustrated in Figure 2.1 with reference to 'community capacity building', an often controversial term that has a close relationship with asset-based approaches. Throughout the text when we use the word 'community' we mean communities of place, interest, action, practice and circumstance.

Figure 2.1: Community capacity building.

As a key part of, but distinct from, community development, community capacity building is a term increasingly used by a range of public agencies that have a responsibility for, or interest in, encouraging community organisations to have a greater influence over local decisions, to drive forward community initiatives or to represent community interests. It has been described as:

> **Activities, resources and support that strengthen the skills, abilities and confidence of people and community groups to take effective action and leading roles in the development of communities (Skinner, 2006, p. 7).**

In the past, community capacity building has been criticised as being based on a deficit model of the skills and confidence of communities, implying that no capacity exists and that it needs building.

On the other hand, successful community capacity building should be based on an understanding of the assets that communities have, working with local groups to help them understand the decision-making processes and develop their ability to inform and influence decisions that affect them directly or indirectly (SCDC, 2012).

While the concept is intrinsically compelling and intuitively right, the language used to describe this movement or shift has not been settled. This was illustrated from our interviews by the following quotations:

'[It] describes some of the things that we are doing that we were struggling to describe, and I think it's really helpful, the articulation of the ideas and concepts and why they are valuable – I think that is quite hard to nail sometimes.' [community-based project manager]

'We're talking about trust and connecting with people, and transforming their options and self-esteem. People like [name], she runs theatre, she doesn't do an asset-based approach … but yet it's demonstrably about discovering assets and abilities unfold. So we should try and find a language that allows people to understand that that's what they're doing.' [academic]

An asset-based approach is however not a new concept, but it has become more significant as we seek to maximise the social determinants of health, which we will discuss later in the chapter, and to embrace new ways of working to tackle persistent inequalities, particularly in challenging economic times.

As we consider how to work differently to improve outcome for individuals it is important to remember that many factors influence how 'healthy' an individual is. Health status is a product of an interaction between societal, environmental, socioeconomic, biological and lifestyle factors, all of which can be modified by healthcare and other policies (OECD, 2011). Taken together these factors can determine whether a person becomes ill or remains healthy, and highlights that the concept of health is broad and an overarching one, and that health affects many aspects of life.

However, today, many of the health problems of greatest concern are considered to be of a different nature to those we have successfully managed in the past, such as infectious diseases. It has been argued that many health problems (e.g. obesity, problematic drug and alcohol use, suicide and violence) are now cultural in origin and character as much as they are results of structural or material factors (Hanlon and Carlisle, n.d.). Such problems and concerns are now often referred to as 'dis-eases' (rather than diseases) because they reflect our individual consciousness, beliefs and motivations that are struggling to cope with modern life (Hanlon and Carlisle, n.d.). It has been proposed that these diseases are a product of life today, in that they are an emergent consequence of the very nature of the lives we have created for ourselves.

What is an 'asset'?

While not ignoring or denying that people have needs, an asset-based approach starts from the premise that individuals and communities also have knowledge, connections, capacity and resources that can be mobilised in order to produce better outcomes. Asset-based practitioners focus on asking the question 'what makes us healthy?' rather than the deficit-based question 'what makes us ill?'. This is often a different approach from other health and care professionals, and has the aim of enhancing people's life chances by focusing on what improves their health and well-being and reducing health inequalities. Assets are realised, expressed, mobilised and sustained through people's actions, connections and participation (Hopkins and Rippon, 2015) and are found at individual, community and organisational levels. A health asset has been defined in the literature as:

any factor or resource which enhances the ability of individuals, communities and populations to maintain and sustain health and well-being and to help to reduce health inequalities. These assets can operate at the level of the individual, family or community and population as protective and promoting factors to buffer against life's stresses (Morgan and Ziglio, 2007, p. 18).

ЖAssets can therefore be described as the collective resources that individuals, families and communities have at their disposal, which protect against negative health outcomes and promote health and well-being and improve life chances.ЖThe primary focus is on valuing individual and collective psychosocial attributes (Friedli, 2012a), including self-esteem, aspiration, confidence, meaning and purpose, optimism and sense of coherence.ЖIt also includes the intangible assets such as knowledge, experience, skills and social capital, that is the links, shared values and understandings in society that enable people and groups to trust each other and work together (Harrison *et al.*, 2004; Lindström and Eriksson, 2009; Foot and Hopkins, 2010; O'Leary *et al*, 2011). Ж

At individual level

An individual's assets are described as being both innate and acquired, their genes and genetic disposition, their own inherent values and beliefs and their life experiences (Rotegard *et al.*, 2010). These assets and internal resources are part of every person, but they are not necessarily recognised or used purposefully or mindfully. The literature supports the assertion that assets, either internal or external, can be harnessed and utilised in challenging situations, but how and if they are used depends on the individual (Rotegard *et al.*, 2010). This point is further reinforced by the quote from a public health academic:

> 'We're talking about trust and connecting people with people, and transforming their options and self-esteem.' [academic]

At organisational level

Organisations, public bodies and services also have assets that can be used to improve well-being – including buildings, land, money, green spaces, employment opportunities, skills, power and voice. These assets are often used to meet immediate needs rather than to sustain the things that make us healthy. Conventional approaches to the delivery of public services are based on meeting needs, providing care and the treatment of presenting problems (Burns, 2013). Services are often delivered in ways that undermine and disempower individuals' and families' capabilities (Hopkins and Rippon, 2015). In doing so they tend to make people passive recipients of services (Foot and Hopkins, 2010) and to build dependency on services.

At community level

Across the UK, over the last decade, the debates about assets at a community level have predominantly focused on physical assets such as community buildings, sports facilities, allotments, forestry or land. References to assets in regeneration policy and recent Scottish legislation on community empowerment focus on the transfer of public assets into community control and community ownership: see for example the Community Empowerment (Scotland) Act 2015 (Scottish Parliament, 2015a).

In *Appreciating Assets* (O'Leary *et al.*, 2011), the International Association for Community Development and the Carnegie UK Trust draw on the seven capitals framework (financial, built, social, human, natural, cultural, political) to describe the range of assets that should be considered interdependently at community level. They suggest that tangible (physical) assets need to be drawn together with 'intangible assets' such as human and social capital, to drive forward community development. They assert that:

> it is people, and not buildings that are the core asset of communities. It is the skills of people who will see that projects can be accomplished. It is people who can learn to see opportunities where before all seemed lost (O'Leary *et al.*, 2011, p. 7).

Both approaches are therefore complementary to one another and, when taken together, reflect a community development approach. Community development seeks to un-tap and mobilise the human capital, the skills, knowledge, experience and social and personal attributes possessed by individuals, which exist within every community, to create strong social and community networks. It supports people to organise around the issues that affect them, their families and communities, and helps them to implement locally led solutions using the whole range of assets they may have available to them (human, social, physical, cultural, political). The process of community development brings all of the assets that lie within communities together to create a force and a vehicle for social change.

According to Foot and Hopkins (2010), assets across these three levels – individual, organisational and community – can therefore be understood in the following ways by recognising the:

- practical skills, capacity and knowledge of people;
- passions and interests of people that give the energy to change;
- networks and connections in a community;
- effectiveness of local community and voluntary associations;
- physical and economic resources of public, private and third sector organisations that are available to support a community;
- physical and economic resources of local places that enhance well-being;
- stories, culture and heritage of the local people and local places.

With these in mind, asset-based approaches are said to offer a coherent set of ideas and concepts for identifying and enhancing the protective factors that help individuals and communities maintain and enhance their health and well-being even when faced with adverse life circumstances. Asset-based approaches offer a relevant and effective way to sustain health-giving assets and support families and communities to mobilise their resources for well-being (Foot, 2012). Working this way requires agencies and communities to invest in actions that build and nurture health-giving assets, prevent illness and benefit the whole community by reducing health inequalities and the steepness of the social gradient in health, as illustrated in Figure 2.2. The defining themes of asset-based ways of working are that they are place-based, relationship-based and citizen-led, and they promote social justice and equality (Foot and Hopkins, 2010).

Figure 2.2: CASE STUDY – Children's Inclusion Partnership (CHIP), North Glasgow

---

Over the past twenty years large parts of the north Glasgow area have been subject to demolition and regeneration, with associated disruption to family and community life. Developed as a partnership between Stepping Stones for Families and Barnardo's, CHIP uses a community development approach, as described below, to enables families and children to:

○   think about what is going on in their communities;
○   speak out about it;
○   achieve positive change as a result.

Communities feel stronger and more optimistic through influencing the circumstances and decisions that affect them:

> **'The model and the process is really key to what we do and how we do it, we apply a community development process to situations where we are asked to help to produce positive outcomes for children and families.' [community development practitioner]**

Working alongside children, families and young people, CHIP staff give local families support, opportunities and a voice in tackling the effects of poverty and disadvantage in their lives through events and programmes delivered throughout the year. CHIP has a vision of working to ensure that all children and young people have an enjoyable life in a healthy, fair and safe environment where they are respected and supported to reach their full potential:

> **'Instead of our project simply "doing it" and putting it on for local people, the approach we took was, "let's make it a partnership thing, let's find out what your ideas are" … so there was a sense in which these were … they felt very much locally owned, these activities.' [community development practitioner]**

Source: http://www.ssff.org.uk/glasgow/children%E2%80%99s-inclusion-partnership
(accessed 11 January 2016)

Theoretical underpinnings

Fundamental to the assets perspective is a focus on health and well-being and the factors that enable and protect health, rather than on illness and individual risk factors of disease. Asset-based approaches draw on a number of perspectives to help us understand the causes and mechanisms of inequities in health, the systematic differences in the health status of different population groups, and potential solutions (GCPH, 2011). Notably, salutogenesis – put forward by

Antonovsky (1993) as a theory to guide health promotion and public health – is a key focus and driver of the approach.

By definition salutogenesis provides a positive view of how health can be created, and helps to identify the skills and resources that people have that positively impact on their health and well-being (see Figure 2.3), particularly on mental well-being (Eriksson and Lindström, 2006). It also helps people manage and cope with difficult situations and challenges throughout their life. Salutogenesis is said to complement the more pathogenic model that emphasises illness and disease. However, when protective factors such as security, consistency, nurture and poverty are absent in the early years, there is evidence to suggest that this has a negative impact on brain structure and function (Krishnadas *et al.*, 2013), especially in relation to language, memory and decision-making abilities as adults (Noble *et al.*, 2015)

Figure 2.3: Asset and resource concepts under the salutogenic umbrella (courtesy of Lindström, Eriksson and Wikström, 2010).

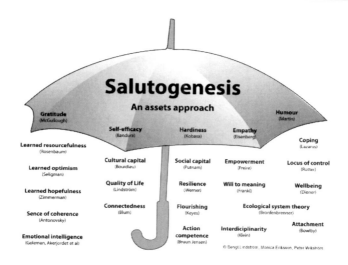

Figure 2.3 explains why some people remain well despite being in stressful situations, while others do not. They have what Antonovsky calls a 'sense of coherence' (Antonovsky and Sagy, 1986; Lindström and Eriksson, 2005), that is, they have ability to understand the world around them and are able successfully to

manage the stresses encountered throughout life. The importance of viewing health in this way is further articulated in the quote below from one of our interviewees:

> '... the focus is on creating wellness. Not necessarily well-being, because well-being is anchored in a kind of medical, health literature. But wellness across all domains of society ... like wellness in terms of educational attainment, engagement with the jobs market, and non-engagement with criminality and drugs and all that kind of thing. Wellness in terms of the way you build relationships. Just people feeling good in everything they do. So how do we create that?' [academic]

An evidence base is available that links this central construct to a range of health-related outcomes (Eriksson and Lindström, 2006). Furthermore, as a validated measurement scale is available (Antonovsky, 1993), it provides an intermediary indicator to gauge an individual's propensity to be in control of their own destiny (A. Morgan, 2014). An individual's sense of coherence is reported to develop throughout their life, but mainly in the first decade, giving support to the policy objectives of 'giving every child the best start in life' (Scottish Government, 2008, p. 10) and 'enabling young people to maximize their capabilities and have control over their lives' (Marmot, 2010, p. 104). However, while the salutogenic model of working provides us with a theory through which we can understand how health comes about and can be maintained, there is little evidence at present of how salutogenic concepts can be put to good use in policies to help people and communities (GCPH, 2011).

Community-led health

Asset-based approaches for health improvement also relate to a community-led health approach, which in turn relates to the wider concept of community development, as described earlier in this chapter. A community-led approach for health improvement is focused on supporting communities experiencing disadvantage and poor health outcomes to identify and define what is important to them about their health and well-being, the factors that impact on their well-being, so they can take the lead in identifying and implementing solutions. A community-led approach for health improvement aims to address health inequalities by enhancing the level of control and influence that disadvantaged communities have over the factors that impact on health and well-being (SCDC, n.d.).

A community-led approach for health improvement has informed the work of community health initiatives in the UK for many years and is the approach to health improvement and addressing inequality that is advocated by the World Health Organization (WHO); it also underpins international policy and practice frameworks for health promotion (WHO, 1986).

A way of thinking about the world

Fundamentally and importantly, and drawing together the discussion and premise of this chapter, an asset-based approach is a set of values and principles and a way of thinking about the world. Proponents would say that a change in the way of seeing the world – 'seeing it as a glass half full rather than half empty' – transforms what we do. Thus an asset-based approach:

- ○ identifies and makes visible the health-enhancing assets in a community;
- ○ sees people and communities as the co-producers of health and well-being, rather than the recipients of services;
- ○ starts with what is working and what people care about, working with people – 'doing with' them, rather than 'doing to' them;
- ○ helps people to identify and focus on the assets and strengths within themselves and their communities, supporting them to make sustainable improvements in their lives;
- ○ supports people to make changes for the better by enhancing skills for resilience, relationships, knowledge and self-esteem;
- ○ supports the building of mutually supportive networks and friendships, which help people make sense of their environments and take control of their lives;
- ○ values what works well in an area;
- ○ identifies what has the potential to improve health and well-being;

○ empowers communities to control their futures and create
   tangible resources such as services, funds and buildings.

The principles of this way of working in practice are further illustrated and effectively summed up in the quote below from a community development manager, working in the community and
voluntary sector:

> 'The key principles would be that, first of all, you need to
> know the community that you're working with, I mean
> know the presenting culture but also the sub-culture, so
> that people get under the skin of a community and under-
> stand the relationships and the networks and how people
> access or don't access, in this case, health services. The next
> principle would be around the need to build relationships
> with people so that you're working with them on a positive
> footing. There's a whole range of principles and it's trying
> to work out the ones you would apply to different sets of
> circumstances and characteristics within a community'.
> [community development manager]

The tensions of using the word 'approach' implies the possibility
of 'people thinking there is a recipe out there' [academic] which they
can just lift off the shelf and implement. However, although the term
may be interpreted in different ways, the lack of an agreed definition
should not be an obstacle in embedding and adopting these underpinning values. The name may change, but the journey of thinking
differently and the potential for transformative change need to continue to enable the benefits of working differently to be realised.

Highlighting the challenges

Challenges and criticisms of these principles and the wider approach
have been put forward and continue to be questioned and examined
(Friedli, 2012a; 2012b; Fischbacher *et al.*, 2013). These points have
been in relation to the approach disregarding:

○ structural and material inequalities;
○ the unequal existing power dynamics in society;
○ the absence of the evidence of effective impact;
○ the low status of the evidence that is available and concerns

about the ability to measure and evaluate the approach robustly;

○ the approach is a money-saving exercise due to the financial climate and context in which it came to the fore.

However, as presented in the quote below from a community-based project manager, awareness of the criticisms about the approaches is an important consideration when working in an asset-based way:

'Being aware of the criticism doesn't mean that it renders the ideas and concepts behind asset-based approaches, you know, null and void. I think being aware of them helps you use them appropriately.' [community-based project manager]

These challenges are not discussed in depth here but are considered and discussed throughout this text as a whole.

Working in an asset-based way is not the missing answer to tackling inequalities, improving health and well-being and achieving positive outcomes for individuals, communities and the population as a whole. That said, careful attention needs to be paid to ensure that it does not divert attention away from broader structural and social issues. Given the criticisms and perceived weaknesses of the approach highlighted above, it could be argued that, with the right investment and commitment and the proper local and national support, this way of working and change in approach to how we work will benefit people and communities in the long run and will lead to a reduced need for expensive public services and will help in achieving a better balance between service delivery and community building (Foot and Hopkins, 2010).

Spot the difference: Asset-based approaches, community development or strengths-based approaches

As highlighted earlier, asset-based approaches and community development have distinct parallels. They are recognised as an integral part of an approach in which both are concerned with bringing people and communities together to achieve positive change using their own knowledge, skills and lived experience around the issues they encounter in their own lives (SCDC, 2011). Asset-based approaches respect that sustained positive health and social out-comes will occur only when people and communities have oppor-tunities and facility to control and manage their own futures. This way of working in practice is further illustrated in the quote below from a community development manager:

> 'For community development workers, it's how we work with individuals within community groups. So, we need to think about the conditions that we can introduce to enable people to bring out the skills, the contacts, the expertise that they have, in relation to themselves, their family and their wider community.' [community development manager]

In a social services context, asset-based approaches are more com-monly known and recognised as strengths-based approaches – the terms themselves are often used interchangeably. A strengths-based approach is based on a way of working with individuals, families and groups, which recognise the importance of the multiple con-texts that influence people's lives (Saint-Jacques *et al.*, 2009; Pattoni, 2012). This perspective focuses on the potentials, strengths, interests, abilities, knowledge and capacities of individuals, rather than their limits. It concerns itself principally with the quality of the relationship that develops between those providing and those being supported, as well as the elements that the person seeking support brings to the process. It is inherently person-centred and is similar to asset-based approaches through being underpinned by the same principles, with empowerment as a central theme. It is most clearly associated with personal co-production (this is explained in more detail in Chapter 3), as opposed to community co-production, which has more empha-sis on collectivism and broader societal value.

A human rights-based approach also sits collectively within these ways of working, which place a central focus on principles of partici-pation, empowerment, non-discrimination and accountability (Alli-ance Scotland, 2013), the importance of which is exemplified in the quote below from an NGO manager:

> 'We don't start off seeing [young people] as a set of prob-lems. I think it is what I have said – it's about seeing people as

whole human beings and believing in the potential capacity for change. I think it's about taking a rights-based approach, that this is about helping young people access their rights to live a life that we would all accept was a good life, and to have services that are tailored to meet that – rather than trying to fit them into services where you are setting them up to fail.' [NGO manager]

A human rights-based approach is the process by which human rights can be protected by adherence to the underlying core values of fairness, respect, equality, dignity and autonomy (or FREDA) (Curtice and Exworthy, 2010). This way of working means integrating human rights norms and principles in the design, implementation, monitoring and evaluation of health-related policies and programmes (WHO, n.d.). In relation to health and healthcare it is based on the understanding that ignoring or violating an individual's human rights has a detrimental effect on their health and well-being and, conversely, using this approach and embedding these values can improve health outcomes and deliver better-quality, person-centred care (Curtice and Exworthy, 2010).

Conclusion

Across perspectives, professions and terminology, asset-based approaches are focused on recognising, valuing and making the most of people's strengths, with a corresponding shift in focus from defining people in terms of what they do not have (their needs) to what they do have (their assets). Asset-based working is not however just another public health 'intervention', nor is it 'the community bit around the edges' (Gamsu, 2015). It involves a paradigm shift in thinking about the health and well-being of individuals, families and communities based on a set of values and principles.

While the idea and principles behind asset-based approaches have been around in some shape and form for a number of decades, the momentum has continued to build in Scotland since 2010 in relation to working and thinking differently. In this chapter we have reflected, discussed and presented thinking on issues of definition and language that surround, promote and often limit the approach. This chapter also raised a number of questions that require further debate and which we will consider in forthcoming chapters. These include: a discussion of whether asset-based approaches are underpinned by a set of principles; how can we ensure that these are embedded and extended across systems and services; what are the implications for practice; and how do we inspire new kinds of practice, foster innovation and share this learning?

Definitions and language are important. But the move towards an asset-based approach needs to be more than just a change in words; otherwise there is a danger of assuming that the right words and intentions will be followed by the right actions.

In the next chapter we summarise the different types of outcomes that asset-based approaches can achieve at different levels, and provide a series of illustrative case examples, which describe the approach in action.

PART 2

The Role of Asset-Based Approaches

CHAPTER 3

What Difference Do Asset-Based Approaches Make?

Introduction

Outcomes are the changes and effects that happen as a result of the action we take. They are a way of describing the difference that is made for individuals, groups, families, organisations or communities arising from a process designed to lead to change.

In the last chapter we attempted to describe what 'assets' and 'asset-based approaches' were and what this way of working meant in practice. In this chapter we outline the differences we might expect from working in asset-based ways and the kinds of outcomes that can be achieved through this way of working at individual, group and community level. We consider the changes asset-based approaches can lead to at institutional and governance levels and highlight the challenges in embedding this approach across systems. Throughout the chapter we reflect on the importance of the participation of individuals and communities in planning for outcomes and evaluating success.

We use quotes from our interviewees to describe a range of perspectives on what differences asset-based approaches make. We present one case study (see Figure 3.1) describing the outcomes achieved for individuals through an asset-based approach to self-management and two further case studies (see Figures 3.4 and 3.5) to illustrate the positive outcomes that have been achieved for individuals and groups through learning and community-led action.

What differences do asset-based approaches make for people and communities?

The use of outcomes as a way to measure progress or improvement is a distinct departure from a target or output-driven system, which focuses on describing success mainly through the use of numerical data: for example, the number of people who attend a community group; or the number of people receiving housing support. While the generation of numerical data is an important indicator of efficacy, a move away from concentrating singularly on the inputs, processes and outputs of activity towards paying attention to the individual experience of individuals and communities enables practitioners to be concerned with the difference that supports are making to people's lives (Cook and Miller, 2012).

Although there are many structural changes and various interventions needed to tackle the impacts of health and social inequalities at population level, there are a number of positive outcomes that can be linked to the use of asset-based approaches, which recognise, mobilise and build on the strengths, capacities, skills and potential of individuals and communities. As far back as the turn of the century the Social Policy Research Unit (SPRU) (Qureshi, 2001) identified the following categories of outcomes as important to people using social services, all of which are still highly relevant today:

- ○ Quality of Life or maintenance outcomes are the aspects of a person's whole life that they are working to achieve or maintain.
- ○ Process outcomes relate to the experience that individuals have in seeking, obtaining and using services and supports.
- ○ Change outcomes are improvements in physical, mental or emotional functioning that individuals are seeking from services or support.

Outcomes are usually measured through the use of a range of indicators (including numerical data as referred to above). Outcome indicators define the evidence to be collected to measure progress and to enable actual results achieved over time to be compared with planned results. They are also measures that describe how well outcomes are being achieved and whether things are changing in the way intended.

In order to provide evidence of how far the use of asset-based approaches can be attributed to the achievement of certain outcomes, indicators associated with the use of the approach need to be set at the stage at which an intervention, or course of action, is planned. If an asset-based approach is at the core of an intervention or change process, all parties (agencies, communities and/or individuals) should be involved from the beginning in planning the outcome's improvement process. In this way, the indicators of success are more likely to reflect the differences individuals, groups and communities know they need. Working in this way also ensures that useful and appropriate evidence is gathered (the use of evidence in relation to asset-based approaches is discussed in detail in Chapter 4).

In the context of health, social services and in community development, asset-based working seeks to support people and communities to maintain or improve health and well-being at individual, group and population level. Well-being, in itself, is seen as an overarching outcome that allows people to realise their aspirations, satisfy their own and their families' needs, and to cope with their own environments in order to live a long, productive and fruitful life (this is discussed in the context of 'salutogenic theory' in Chapter 2).

Well-being and improved health are often described as broad, or end, outcomes. There are many other and varied outcomes that will ultimately lead to improved health and well-being (sometimes described as intermediate outcomes). These will be of importance to different people, groups and communities at various stages in their lives and circumstances, and have been neatly summed up by one interviewee:

> 'I think the outcomes people seek vary according to their own different circumstances and their own pathways through life.' [NGO manager]

A number of outcomes associated with taking an asset-based approach have been proposed for individuals and communities (GCPH, 2012). Potential changes include: more control over their lives and where they live; the ability to influence decisions that affect them and their communities; the opportunity to be engaged in whatever aspects of community and social life they might want to be; and the wish to be seen as part of the solution, not the problem. The hypothesis is that those changes may then lead to increased well-being through strengthening control, influence, knowledge and self-esteem, extension of social contacts and networks, and the development of skills for life and work – as outlined by a community development manager:

'We need to work with people where they are not seen as a problem that needs to be fixed. The problem lies with the structures and the systems that have created poor conditions for people. The fundamental value base underpinning asset based approaches must be about empowerment of people to change their own circumstances and work with others to influence change towards improved outcomes at structural level.' [community development manager]

The outcomes demonstrated above describe a range of changes for individuals, groups, communities and organisations linked to asset-based ways of working – but how might those outcomes come about? Although there is promising literature about asset-based approaches in a range of contexts and at different levels (individual, group and community), to date it tends to focus on the process and change outcomes of adopting the approach, rather than the quality of life outcomes that are achieved (Voorberg *et al.*, 2014; Findlay, 2015).

The rest of this chapter attempts to bring together the limited sources of published research, grey literature and case study examples, from which the emerging evidence of the kinds of outcomes that can be expected to be achieved through adopting asset-based approaches at these different levels. Case studies are used to outline the role and practice of asset-based approaches in helping to achieve the outcomes described. It should be noted that much of this material is fragmented and to date there remain significant gaps that require to be addressed (the particular difficulties of measuring asset-based approaches is discussed in Chapter 4). Indeed a large proportion of the available evidence base calls for the development of a more systematic approach to measuring and demonstrating asset-based approaches (GCPH, 2012; Baker, 2014; Tobi *et al.*, 2014; Alvarez-Dardet *et al.*, 2015).

Outcomes at the individual level

At the individual level, as discussed in Chapter 2, asset-based approaches – particularly within the context of social services – are close to and often synonymous with strengths-based practice.

Strengths-based practice is a move away from a narrow focus on the limitations of people and a preoccupation with 'problems', 'treatment' and 'case management'. Instead, strengths-based practice involves enabling a person to locate, articulate and build upon their individual assets or capabilities (sometimes termed their 'inner resources'), with an emphasis on what they can do, not what they cannot (Staudt *et al.*, 2001; Saleebey, 2006; Pulla, 2012). The premise is that, regardless of previous experience or history, everybody has something valuable to contribute. In this way this approach can be seen to link closely to the theories of 'recovery', 'person-centred practice', 'self-management' and 're-ablement' – terms that are familiar to many working in health and social services.

At the individual level, an example of the asset-based approach is 'individualised' or 'personal' co-production (Griffiths and Foley, 2009). This is a form of co-production that is focused on the relationship between the person and the provider and as such could be considered easier to implement than other forms of co-production (such as peer-based work) (Findlay, 2015). This form of co-production is more closely aligned with the 'personalisation' agenda in social services, which generates value directly for the individual, although some authors contend that collective value may also be generated in some circumstances (see for example Alford, 2009). Findlay (2015, p. 1) suggests in a recent analytical review that the empirical evidence across Europe is 'dominated by individualised forms of co-production', rather than collective co-production.

What does the published evidence show?

With this in mind, it is evident that asset-based approaches can range from the abstract to the extremely specific. A recent empirical review of the research on strengths-based approaches highlighted a lack of a clear description for the underlying intervention (Ibrahim *et al.*, 2014). The omission on the nature of the intervention made the synthesis of evidence difficult, because of the plethora of different interventions, populations and issues that were examined in the literature. For example, although strengths-based practice has been prominent in the context of mental health (Saleebey, 2006), it has been extended and shown to be applicable in a range of contexts including: older adults (Chapin *et al.*, 2006); substance misuse (Staudt *et al.*, 2001); and families (Early and Glenmaye, 2000).

The benefits to individuals across this range of settings include the promotion of hope, empowerment and attainment of personal goals. These are described in more detail below.

The promotion of hope

Francis (2014, p. 269) states that:

> by engaging with clients with a sense of hope and a belief that people can change, social workers can work with the client to identify a sense of purpose for their life, create a sense of belonging, and develop a sense of hope.

It is this underpinning feature of strengths-based practice, like that of asset-based approaches, that is thought to enable people to look beyond their immediate concerns and supports them to conceive of a future that inspires them, providing confidence that their circumstances can improve (Pulla, 2012).

Strengths-based approaches are shown to be effective in developing and maintaining hope in individuals, and consequently many studies cite evidence for enhanced well-being and recovery (Smock *et al.,* 2008; Park and Peterson, 2006). For example, in their review, Early and Glenmaye (2000) found that the use of a strengths-based perspective in families not only helped families identify resources for coping, but also encouraged use of existing strengths to sustain hope and a sense of purpose by setting and achieving goals in line with their personal aspirations, capabilities and visions of a possible life. In a review of fifty-six programmes MacLeod and Nelson (2000) similarly found evidence to support the view that an empowerment approach is critical in interventions for vulnerable families.

To illustrate this further, an example of a strengths-based method of working at the individual and group level is demonstrated in Figure 3.1.

Figure 3.1: CASE STUDY – Wellness Recovery Action Planning

Wellness Recovery Action Planning (WRAP) is an approach that has been developed by Mary Ellen Copeland, who established the Copeland Centre based in Arizona, USA. WRAP promotes a structured approach to self-management in recovery using the five key notions of hope, personal responsibility, education, self-advocacy and support. The aim is to empower individuals to take control through the use of a range of strategies and development of action plans to improve their well-being. Although the approach has been predominantly used in mental health, it can be used for a variety of people in different circumstances.

The focus from the outset is on 'wellness', not 'illness', and the structured process of thinking and acting in this way is considered to enable the development of self-awareness, reflection on certain behaviours or thoughts, and active planning that contributes to well-being. It is this emphasis on self-management and recovery that resonates well with the asset-based approach, particularly in terms of empowering people to manage their own health and conditions.

Outcomes

A recent evaluation of WRAP in groups found that the approach, when delivered by trained facilitators who could share their lived experience, was considered to be very relevant, effective and had substantial and positive impact on those who had been part of the process. This impact was sustained over time.

A more recent feasibility study for a proposed randomised control trial (RCT) comparing WRAP with mindfulness-based cognitive therapy (MBCT) found that:

○ WRAP had a major positive impact on mental well-being;
○ those with experience of other treatments tended to say that WRAP was better, although it could be used in conjunction with medication;
○ the support and advice of those with similar lived experiences made the WRAP approach particularly powerful (MacGregor *et al.*, 2014).

Source: adapted from Pratt et al., 2013.

Empowerment and attainment of personal goals

It is considered that the practitioner role in supporting people to change their own (often) negative narratives of themselves, by encouraging them to explore and acknowledge alternatives, is a crucial feature of strengths-based practice (Walther and Fox, 2012 as cited in Helmer *et al.*, 2014). Many of the positive outcomes of strengths-based interventions are often attributed to the development of positive relationships between those being supported and those providing support.

The strengths-based approach is hinged upon a shared responsibility between the person and the practitioner in considering opportunities for change and pathways to improved outcomes. In this way strengths-based practice concerns itself principally with the quality of the relationship that develops between those providing and being supported, as well as the elements that the person seeking support brings to the process (Duncan and Miller, 2000). As such, the power relationship between a person who is supported and the person doing the supporting is negotiated. Working within this refreshed relationship, practitioners respect the person's decision about what is or is not helpful for their journey towards improved personal outcomes, making sure the person is enabled to make informed choices (Chapin *et al.*, 2015).

The evidence shows that encouraging people who are supported by services to focus on determining their own pathways and having greater involvement in service delivery can lead to higher levels of satisfaction because of greater 'moral ownership' and adapting services to personal needs (Verschuere *et al.*, 2012). This is consistent with other social work research highlighting that the therapeutic relationship between practitioners and those supported by services instil enhanced feelings of responsibility and self-efficacy (Newlin *et al.*, 2015). For example, in a review with individuals participating in strengths-based case management, people identified feeling free to talk about both strengths and weaknesses as important for helping them to set goals that they wanted to achieve and to make changes to their lives (Brun and Rapp, 2001). As such, researchers have postulated that the value of setting self-defined goals may be more likely to be achieved, as the individuals themselves have directed their development.

Some empirical analyses have also suggested that strengths-based approaches may encourage people to stay involved in treatment programmes, most notably in the context of substance misuse (Rapp *et al.*, 1998). In a comparison between different types of case management, researchers found that strengths-based case management was effective in increasing the use of community-based services, retention in treatment programmes and improving quality of life and satisfaction from those supported (Vanderplasschen *et al.*, 2007). Although these positive effects were highlighted, researchers also cautioned that outcomes relating to reduction in drug use and improvements in psychosocial function were less consistent.

Figure 3.2 provides an overview of the different types of outcomes that have been identified through adopting asset-based approaches and a strengths-based approach at the individual level (Morgan and Ziglio, 2007; Pulla, 2012; South, 2015).

Figure 3.2: Individual level outcomes.

Improved personal resilience

- ○ increased health literacy and life skills – increased knowledge, awareness, skills and capabilities;
- ○ higher self-esteem;
- ○ healthier lifestyle leading to improved health and well-being;
- ○ sense of purpose;
- ○ increased confidence and self-efficacy;
- ○ improved social relationships and social support, reduced isolation;
- ○ improved retention in therapeutic programmes.

Discussion in this chapter so far outlines the kind of evidence that is becoming available to support the case for asset-based working. However it is also important to assess alternative perspectives. As recently as 2009, there has been commentary about the apparent scarcity of research evaluating the efficacy of strengths-based practice of any kind (Lietz, 2009). For example, a systematic review in 2014 examining the evidence from clinical trials focused on determining the impact of strengths-based approaches in people with severe mental illness; these found no significant difference between strengths-based approaches adopted and the other service delivery models in terms of level of every day functioning and quality of life (Ibrahim *et al.*, 2014). The researchers highlighted the need for further evidence because of the low number of trials included within the sample (including randomised controlled trials/RCTs and quasi experimental studies), further reinforcing the position that more must be done to establish firm evidence for asset-based approaches at each of the respective levels.

Outcomes at group and community level

Individuals belong within families, networks and communities, and it is important to ensure that the assets of associations – the knowledge about and interactions with family, social networks and communities – are valued and built upon. Working in a group or at a collective level offers a different route to achieving improved outcomes both for the individual and the groups and communities they belong to. There is an important distinction between some of the outcomes that can be expected for people through an individualised approach and those that can be expected for individuals through using asset-based approaches at the collective level:

> ... the collective approach not only builds trust and improves relationships between service users and service providers, but also contributes to more cohesive communities and offers new channels for the creation of social capital (Griffiths and Foley, 2009, p. 5).

For many health, social care and community development practitioners, the concept of group approaches to change is fundamental to practice. People coming together over a common issue or concern, or common bonds and affinities, can lead to improved outcomes at personal, family, group, community and societal level. As discussed in Chapter 1, structural change is not achieved by the act of individuals or policy initiatives alone, but instead comes about mainly through collective action, as exemplified by the disability or trade union movements.

Findlay (2015, p.14) however highlights that the nature of the available literature on collective co-production is 'problematic as it makes it difficult to draw conclusions about causality or measure the impact that involvement in co-production initiatives can have on people and community outcomes'. This review distinguishes between evidence of 'intrinsic benefits' (that the process is useful and productive in and of itself) and evidence of 'instrumental benefits' (the value people get through improved outcomes because of the approach taken).

Furthermore Parrado *et al.* (2013), in a study using data from a large sample survey across five European countries, reported that self-efficacy – the feeling that individual action can have an impact on political and social change – was the most important driver of collective co-production. Voorberg *et al.* (2014, p. 16) argue however that 'we do not know if co-production/co-creation contributes to outcomes which really address the needs of citizens in a robust way'.

Figure 3.3 provides an overview of the different types of outcomes that have been reported through adopting asset-based approaches and collective co-production at group and community levels (Morgan and Ziglio, 2007; GCPH, 2012).

Figure 3.3: Group and community-level outcomes.

- increased social networks;
- sense of affinity and belonging;
- increased trust between individuals and groups;
- community cohesion;
- intergenerational solidarity;
- religious tolerance and harmony;
- improved physical environment;
- improved community facilities and resources;
- partnership working between groups and between groups and agencies;
- increased influence.

Although many groups are self-organising, people who are marginalised or who experience the impacts of poor health and structural health and social inequalities often need support to come together to create peer-support systems and to provide a space where they can work together to engage in different forms of social action. Figure 3.4 illustrates an asset-based approach at group and community level and highlights the importance of bring people together to support them to develop their skills, build their own social networks and make an effective contribution within their community.

Figure 3.4: CASE STUDY – GalGael Trust.

GalGael provides learning experiences anchored in practical activities that offer purpose and meaning. The work of the trust is founded on the belief that everyone has something to contribute to the local economy and their local community. Working with adults who are long-term unemployed, many of whom experience complex and often multiple forms of deprivation and exclusion, GalGael provides a space and a workplace that challenges, inspires and creates the conditions conducive to learning – a space where issues are left at the door and new positive identities forged:

> **'Having a relational approach is important to our ability to engage people and sustain that engagement.' [community-based project manager]**

The Journey On programme delivered by GalGael seeks to reconnect people with the best within themselves through positive learning journeys grounded in hands-on practical activities, such as working on producing wooden products, working alongside crafts-people to handcraft furniture, cooking, processing Scottish timber or helping at public events:

> **'Useful learning happens in experiential situations as opposed to classroom settings ... it is about saying where are the learning opportunities in these real world activities that we are involved in and how do we support people to plot a journey through those, whether it is building new skills or broadening the skills they already have.'** [community-based project manager]

Using traditional skills as a vehicle and working with natural materials such as wood, stone and metal, Journey On provides opportunities to pick up new skills and get into good life habits, thereby creating numerous opportunities for developing personal strengths. When new opportunities arise, individuals are supported to progress as their skills, capabilities and confidence increase. These learning journeys are enriched by wider activities like boatbuilding, rowing, rural skills, community and creative projects. At the benches, people build products and confidence and form the kind of working relationships that will help them in the future. GalGael creates a workplace where individuals can take a lead in their own progression and development.

Source: www.galgael.org (accessed 11 January 2016).

A community development, or a community-led health approach, seeks to support groups to form around their own shared concerns or aspirations, or around a need or gap in services at a local level, with the aim of turning 'private issues into public concerns'. From a community development and health and social care services perspective, assessing and valuing assets alongside addressing needs will help to give a better understanding of the requirements of individuals and communities, and will help to build resilience, increase social capital and enable a shift towards more empowering, sustainable and holistic approaches to delivering services. A further example (see Figure 3.5) demonstrates a community-led approach to achieving more positive outcomes for children with additional support needs, their families and wider community.

Although there are a growing number of examples of the positive outcomes that can be achieved through using an asset-based approach to working with people at individual and group level, it has proved more difficult to find evidence of the outcomes that can

Figure 3.5: CASE STUDY – PAGES (Parent's Advisory Group for Education and Socialisation).

PAGES is based in a rural part of Aberdeenshire in Scotland and grew from a group of parents who faced common challenges in finding appropriate support services for their children and also in accessing suitable help for themselves. PAGES is run by local parents and independently provides support and resources for young people, children and families, which respond directly to their needs, and which otherwise are not accessible in the locality. All activities are designed directly by the people using them and are therefore responsive and flexible to the requirements of existing and new members.

Along with other local groups, PAGES contributes to the running of a vibrant community resource which offers space for groups to meet, a kitchen and eating space, a craft room, broadband access and a community garden. The resource is used by a cross section of people from the community and is fully inclusive. PAGES engages with a wide range of statutory providers to engender a partnership approach to the delivery of local services, which can be influenced and directed by those accessing them. PAGES uses an asset-based approach by putting the people using their services at the centre in designing activities, running events and in taking responsibility for overall management:

> **'Giving somebody something that we know they can do saying: "We are relying on you" helps them realise they have something to offer.' [a parent]**

Outcomes

PAGES has achieved the following outcomes at group and individual level:
○ improved social support networks;
○ reduced isolation and improved social inclusion;
○ improved mental health, well-being and confidence;
○ increased skills and capabilities;
○ a sense of belonging and purpose;
○ more responsive services.

Source: http://www.pagesaberdeenshire.com (accessed 11 January 2016)

be achieved through taking an asset-based approach at community level. As discussed in Chapter 1, in Scotland this may be due to a retraction of neighbourhood-based community development work and an emphasis on physical and economic regeneration, as opposed to social regeneration, in housing policy over the last few decades (GoWell, 2014).

The Link Up programme, delivered by Inspiring Scotland, sought to establish a model of place-based working through adopting asset-based practice in ten local communities in Scotland over a three year period. Its recent evaluation found evidence that the initiative had significant positive personal impacts for those residents who have been actively involved, citing outcomes related to new social networks, increased confidence and skills, more involvement in community activity and improved relationships between different age ranges and cultural groups (ODS Consulting, 2014). In addition to outcomes for individuals, the evaluation also reported that outcomes at the level of the community included: better community integration and cohesion; greater capacity of local people to influence what happens locally; and an improved perception of the area as a place to live. The evaluation stated however that, at the end of the three-year period, the evidence was unable to demonstrate that the positive changes were reaching significantly beyond the actively engaged Link Up participants (ODS Consulting, 2014).

Similar approaches have also been adopted in England. Notably the NHS-funded Health Empowerment Leverage Project (HELP), using a community development method based on asset-based principles in five communities in England over an eighteen-month period. This reported a number of results including:

> more resilient and confident communities, healthier behaviours and improved health outcomes, better informed and responsive services, reduction in health inequalities and cost savings where pressure and spend are greatest (HELP, 2012, as cited in Hopkins and Rippon, 2015).

The HELP approach proposed that:

> increasing the breadth and effectiveness of community-led activity has a number of beneficial effects simultaneously, including giving people greater control over their own lives, enabling them to feel better and be healthier, enables them to cooperate with others to improve their shared conditions; and enables them to participate in dialogue and negotiation with public agencies, making those more accountable and responsive (HELP, 2012).

Although the Link Up and HELP experiences demonstrate a number of positive outcomes for those directly involved, they also recognise that any improved outcomes at neighbourhood level achieved through using a place-based, asset-based community development approach were likely to take a longer period of time to be realised. That said, where there is a commitment to community development at local level over a sustained period, evidence from community development literature and programmes like Link Up may lead us to expect to achieve outcomes such as:

○ active networks of local groups, clubs, societies and informal connections that complement and support the purpose of local government;

○ communities and local voluntary organisations working with local government, as equal partners, to work out the best way to plan and deliver public services, making sure that all interests are brought together to share their understanding and to meet needs as successfully as possible;

○ positive, equal and co-productive relationships between public services and communities;

○ communities as long-term partners in change, where community-based organisations such as housing associations or local development trusts work to increase local participation, alongside securing physical assets such as premises or land to enable communities to generate income to support the delivery of programmes of activity independently;

○ improved local democratic processes at ward level, ensuring that local people and community organisations are active rather than passive, independent rather than dependent, and where political power is shared rather than exercised;

○ improved democratic processes at strategic planning level, between public agency and community interests;

○ a distinct community sector where resident groups, housing associations, development trusts, community centres, social enterprises, credit unions and health initiatives are community-led or community-driven and, where they work in collaboration, shared services and resources or commissions from each other (Garven *et al.*, 2014).

Outcomes at institution and systems level

Current literature around asset-based working advocates that such approaches have the potential to help address Scotland's continuing health problems and can contribute to improving outcomes in innovative ways. While outcomes can be relatively easily described for the individual or for groups, the published evidence of the impact of this way of working, especially at the population level, is scarce. It is recognised however that gathering research on the impact at population level will take time, require long-term investment and a shared vision of what we want support to look and feel like, in order to understand how asset-based approaches will lead to the kinds of outcomes we seek.

As highlighted throughout this chapter, there are a growing number of examples of asset-based working and outcomes that can be achieved for individuals and groups. At the level of organisation, system or population, outcomes associated with this way of working could help reduce health inequalities by impacting on the wider structural determinants of health – by building stronger local economies, by safeguarding the environment and by developing more cohesive communities by making the best use of their resources and maximising their human, physical and financial assets.

When considering the available research in relation to population or organisational assets (GCPH, 2011), it is well established that adult health and health-related behaviours tend to be worse in more disadvantaged areas, after controlling for individual characteristics such as income and education. This has been associated with the premise that environmental characteristics in poorer areas are detrimental to health and healthy living and do not promote physical, social and mental well-being (MacIntyre *et al.*, 1993). Living in safe and pleasant housing has also been recognised as being of benefit not only to the residents but also to the community and wider society (GoWell, 2014), alongside improving community cohesion and connectedness, reducing crime and enhancing employment opportunities and educational achievement (Steptoe and Feldman, 2001). Furthermore organisational-level assets such as volunteering opportunities have been shown to convey individual health benefits, in additional to wider social benefits.

These positive outcomes include enriched life satisfaction and self-esteem, increased sense of purpose, and better self-rated physical and mental health as well as educational and occupational achievement (Wilson, 2000; Post, 2005; Jenkinson *et al.*, 2013). Studies of youth volunteering indicate that volunteering reduces the likelihood of engaging in problem behaviours such as truancy from school and drug abuse (Wilson, 2000). A systematic review has also shown that peer support facilitated positive outcomes for physical activity and smoking cessation (Webel *et al.*, 2010).

Institution- and systems-level outcomes (Morgan and Ziglio, 2007; GCPH, 2011) are shown in Figure 3.6.

Figure 3.6: Institution and systems-level outcomes.

- public health intelligence;
- better policymaking;
- increased opportunities for voluntary service;
- improved access to health and care services, appropriate use of services and culturally relevant services;
- availability and improved access to environmental and physical resources necessary for promoting physical, mental and social health and well-being;
- employment security and opportunities;
- availability of safe and pleasant housing;
- better service reach, uptake of screening and other preventative services;
- co-produced services and outcomes;
- political democracy and social justice.

Interest in the benefits and role of asset-based working for improved outcomes at the level of operating services and systems and at scale within populations continues to grow. However action at this level remains limited, and identification of good practice at this level is challenging. Where it does exist, practice appears to be confined to specialised services for vulnerable target groups delivered on the margins of mainstream delivery (McLean *et al.*, in preparation)) rather than a model of working embraced across services as a whole. Where it does exist, practice is relationship and values-based and is responsive, adaptable and sensitive to an individual's requirements and aspirations, with positive outcomes achieved as presented in the WRAP example (see Figure 3.1). The level of impact of this way of working within services is therefore at present evident for the individual, through the recording of data at small systems level. The impact of asset-based approaches at the level of whole systems remains to be seen.

At the level of the institution, in Scotland the decisive and distinctive approach to delivering policy and public services by national government known as the Scottish Approach to Government (see Chapter 1) highlights the use of asset-based approaches and co-production, underpinned by the improvement framework, as it shifts towards a more engaging and participatory system of governance. This change of focus aims to ensure engagement with the people of Scotland is sustained and empowering; it builds on the strengths and assets of Scotland's communities, organisations and places; and it supports the meaningful involvement of people in designing and delivering new approaches to achieving outcomes and shared ambitions. Although the intention and ambitions of this way of working on a national basis is to be commended, an understanding of how better outcomes can be achieved for people and communities and the population as whole through asset-based approaches remains to be defined.

In an attempt to bridge this gap in evidence in a Scottish context, the Glasgow Centre for Population Health (GCPH) and the Scottish Community Development Centre (SCDC) carried out a programme of action research in a number of areas across Scotland to try to identify how adopting and embedding the characteristics of asset-based working can be taken on more fully at systems level; if existing systems can change to effect tangible and sustainable improvement through alternative approaches; and what improved outcomes might be achieved (GCPH and SCDC, 2015a; 2015b). The research highlighted the importance of long-term local investment, the role of local partnerships to work effectively across sectors, the building of a collective goal or vision, and the need for time for consideration and implementation of new ways of working.

Conclusion

Overall, this chapter served to highlight that people and communities are more likely to achieve positive outcomes if they have exercised their choice as part of the process of planning for change, on either an individual or a group level. Empowerment that comes through having choice, control and the opportunity to contribute can provide long-term gains where people are at the centre of their own care and support, are involved in community life and can engage with public service systems to help them respond more effectively.

However finding compelling evidence that asset-based approaches are directly related to the outcomes described in this chapter remains a challenge. In the next chapter we describe these difficulties in greater detail and question how the evidence base might be strengthened.

CHAPTER 4

Exploring the Nature of Evidence for Asset-Based Approaches

Introduction

There are significant methodological challenges associated with adequately measuring and evidencing asset-based approaches as touched on in the previous chapter. In this chapter we consider these challenges in greater depth and highlight the fact that adoption of asset-based approaches raises the need to reconceptualise how we define and accept evidence, its nature and its role.

We assert that research and evaluation methods that are congruent with the values and principles of asset-based approaches are located in participatory, appreciative and action-oriented practice (Sigerson and Gruer, 2011). Therefore adopting an asset-based approach raises questions such as: 'how can we measure "together"?', 'who decides what we measure?' and 'what is the role of local knowledge compared with systematic reviews of evidence?'. We consider that methods which are able to embrace the complex and messy nature of 'real life', as well as those that explicitly value evidence and knowledge-based practice, are required in order to understand the use and value of asset-based approaches in practice and their link in improving well-being.

This chapter therefore examines what is useful to measure and research at individual, group and societal levels and uses case studies to highlight methods that can aid measurement at each of these levels. Because of the complexity and evolving nature of the evidence for asset-based approaches, in this chapter we discuss subjective well-being as a key measure of progress in achieving better health and social outcomes, while recognising the different conceptualisations between 'personal outcomes important to people using services' and 'wellbeing' (Barrie and Miller, 2015). Quotes from our research interviewees serve to highlight the resonance of these challenges in practice.

What do we measure? A question of value

Prosperity can be broadly defined as 'a successful, flourishing, or thriving condition, especially in financial respects; good fortune' (*Dictionary.com*).

Although nations have traditionally tended to measure success against a number of indicators, in many national comparisons across countries there is a singular focus on Gross Domestic Product (GDP) as the prominent indicator of prosperity. While GDP provides important data on what we produce, what we consume and our income as a society, researchers and organisations are beginning to highlight the limitations of focusing on this measure alone, particularly when considering the distribution of wealth, and what accounts for people's well-being (Stiglitz *et al.*, 2009; Jackson, 2011; Smith and Herren, 2011; Nussbaum, 2011).

What we choose to measure defines what is important and directs where governments focus their energies (Fry, 2009). Therefore moving away from this sole focus on wealth towards a wider definition of prosperity that is inclusive of factors such as health and well-being presents the opportunity for society to reframe and debate what we value, what we aspire to achieve and how we measure progress. This offers the potential to refocus on what matters to people and what outcomes we collectively wish to achieve.

In Scotland, although there is a progressive move towards measuring outcomes and performance on a national level through the national performance framework (as discussed in Chapter 1), this shift towards outcomes is being further advanced by the Carnegie UK Trust and others who promote the focus on quality of life and well-being as key measures of progress. Being considered an important complement to traditional measures, it is argued that both policymakers and wider civil society can use well-being indicators as a way to monitor overall progress and direction as a society, and that measures and analysis of the drivers of well-being should be used to identify policy gaps and issues that are not receiving sufficient attention by policymakers (Wallace, 2013). The development of robust measures of well-being that explicitly value non-material and non-monetary assets are considered essential in ensuring that their significant contribution is counted and valued (Fry, 2009).

Alternative methods of assessing progress

Given the recognition and emphasis on the importance of well-being as a criterion of prosperity, alternative methods of measurement are gaining pace in public discourse. Organisations such as New Economics Foundation (NEF) and Oxfam directly challenge how we consider what counts, and what is worth assessing, at both a national and local level. For example, the five ways to well-being framework provides a set of evidence-based actions, which promote people's well-being (Aked *et al.*, 2008). Similarly the Oxfam Humankind Index was devised as a new way of measuring what makes a good life: one that acknowledges money and material possessions, while also recognising that other factors contribute to developing a prosperous nation. Of critical importance is that this index of prosperity has been developed through direct engagement with citizens and that it emphasises factors such as social capital, health and the physical environment (Oxfam, 2012).

This discourse is also prevalent in other countries across the world where alternative measures are being developed with varying levels of success. These include:

- ❍ Index of Sustainable Economic Welfare (ISEW). This is used in Finland and some US states;
- ❍ Genuine Progress Indicator (GPI) found in Canada and some US states;
- ❍ Human Development Index (HDI) pioneered by the United Nations;
- ❍ Inclusive Wealth Index (IWI). This is a joint collaboration between the United Nations University International Human Dimensions Programme (UNUIHDP) and the United Nations Environment Programme (UNEP).

A recent critique of all of these comparative methods has highlighted that none of the measures set out are perfect and that there is a general need for further refinement of the indicators (Van den Bergh and Antal, 2014). In stating this the authors argue that:

> we should not wait to eliminate or substitute GDP by another measure until a perfect alternative welfare indicator is available. It is unlikely that a single indicator can be

constructed to undo the long list of objections against GDP (Van den Bergh and Antal, 2014, p. 10).

All of the alternative indices recognise the multidimensional nature of well-being and emphasise the need to draw on a variety of different types of evidence in order to reflect accurately what is happening for people.

With their focus on improving well-being, it is clear how asset-based approaches present a good fit with these progressive methods of measurement. Questioning what we value as a society presents a useful proposition to enable the growing debate about how we can co-produce well-being alongside people living and working in communities. This is particularly important given that 'the outcomes from asset-based working should be part of an evidence-based pathway to the high-level public health outcomes of wellbeing and health equity' (Hopkins and Rippon, 2015, p. 28). There are inherent difficulties however in measuring asset-based approaches and understanding their relationship to well-being and positive outcomes for people; these will be outlined in the following sections. This leads to more practical considerations of what is useful to measure at a local level, as well as what type or types of evidence may inform policymaking.

The nature of evidence

Although there are ever more examples of asset-based approaches within communities and within individual practice (McLean and McNeice, 2012; Inglis, 2013; Hopkins and Rippon, 2015), determining how, why and whether they achieve the expressed outcomes of people and communities related to well-being is complex (Ogilvie *et al.*, 2006; Craig *et al.*, 2008). A key feature of this complexity is that asset-based approaches in themselves are inherently contrary to the conventional way that research and evaluation are undertaken. The person-centred, context-focused and emergent nature of asset-based approaches challenge some of the typical questions we usually take for granted around evidence, research and measurement. For example, it leads us to consider:

- ○ who measures?
- ○ what is measurement for?

○ who defines the issues that need attention?

○ who determines the methods that will be used?

○ whose evidence, expertise and experience influences decision-making?

○ when does the approach begin and end?

○ when do we have enough evidence?

○ when is the evidence good enough?

○ who determines the basis on which the evidence constitutes improvement?

The answers to these questions will vary depending on the purpose of measurement at stake, as people, practitioners, communities, funders and policymakers are all relevant actors in producing evidence and making decisions. Fundamentally, working in an asset-based way means seeking to adopt a more relational and evolving process of measurement and evaluation where those who were previously 'researched' become 'co-researchers' or lead researchers (Pearce, 2008). This means that those who are involved in the process are seen as equal partners in the creation of reliable knowledge where 'their interpretations and understandings are as central to the process as the researcher or the practitioner' (Greenwood, 2015, p. 205). This way of working promotes and respects a range of different forms of evidence – taking particular cognisance of that which is rooted in context and generated through discussion with those who are involved. A key example of this is participatory action research (discussed later in this chapter), which is a particular form of inquiry that shares the values of asset-based approaches, seeing action, evaluation and measurement as interlinked.

Although regarded by some as 'lower status' in the hierarchy of evidence (Hunter *et al.*, 2010) and despite the 'renewed skepticism towards "soft" evaluative research, critical accounts (that are viewed, and dismissed as, ideological) and qualitative research' (Durose *et al.*, 2014, p. 7), much of the emerging evidence around asset-based approaches to working with people and improving community circumstances comes from case studies and exploratory primary research. These forms of evidence are particularly relevant to the methods and the values of the approach as will be discussed throughout this chapter.

What counts as 'useful evidence' depends on its purpose; the question the evidence is trying to answer; how it is going to be used; who it is for; and in what environment (Nutley *et al.*, 2013). Indeed it has more recently been stated that 'it is not the lack of evidence that seems to be the issue; rather, it is the lack of the status of the evidence on asset-based approaches' (Hopkins and Rippon, 2015, p. 19). As such, as the commentary and evidence base for asset-based and community development approaches continue to develop, there is an ongoing need for practitioners to share good practice and learning and to 'ensure that the criticisms or perceived weaknesses (the limited evidence base being one) of the approach being taken seriously and that we think of ways of addressing them' (A. Morgan, 2014, p. 4).

Methodological principles underpinning successful evaluation and measurement

Against this background, and given the early stages of research and evaluation of asset-based approaches, it is unsurprising that the evidence for these ideas could be considered fragmented and underdeveloped. As well as the need to improve the evidence base, it is also important to improve the measurement and evaluation methodologies employed to understand the use of the approach in practice. However, there remains a series of complex methodological quandaries for evidencing and measuring asset-based approaches, and there is some recognition in the literature that the evaluation of asset-based working is lagging behind its practice (A. Morgan, 2014). Indeed this was an issue raised by a policymaker during our key informant interviews:

> 'I think we have to have the courage of our conviction that it's right ... The whole problem of how we collect data and what it is we are measuring I think is a very real one for this area, and again we shouldn't underestimate it or be afraid of it.' [policymaker]

In a useful study of 'what works' in the assessment of complex interventions, Coote *et al.* (2004) recommend that for evaluation to be valued and valuable:

- There should be a sustained investment in time and resources to develop evaluation techniques, particularly the best ways of combining multiple methods.
- There needs to be a broad consensus about evaluation standards.
- A more open and extensive dialogue needs to be generated about the challenges of evaluating complex community-based initiatives.
- The value of involving people and practitioners in evaluation needs to be recognised alongside the opportunity for learning from their experience.

Likewise Durose *et al.* (2014, p. 11) suggest that: 'Organisations seeking to evaluate their own co-productive ways of working could do so in ways which are explicit about the underpinning value base.' In the context of asset-based approaches, it follows that appropriate evaluation and research models are those that are focused on understanding complexity, are rooted in context, share the values of discovering and mobilising what people and communities have to offer and are appreciative and collaborative. As such, outlined below are a number of underpinning principles reviewed in the literature that should be considered when choosing an appropriate course of action to evaluate and measure the impact of asset-based approaches.

Embrace the interrelated nature of action, reflection and evaluation

As mentioned previously, it is difficult to separate the 'implementation' and the 'measurement' of asset-based approaches, as they are ultimately interlinked. Asset-based approaches assume ongoing collaboration with people and communities to define, to assess and to take action, which can be considered countercultural to how evaluation or research is ordinarily constructed.

Asset-based approaches recognise the assets of everyone, individually and collectively, and as such external evaluators or researchers are involved, but their perspectives are not favoured over others. The critical point is ensuring that important forms of knowledge and ways of knowing are not neglected because they are different to those that have been created through traditional research (Morton and Wright,

2015). Instead, different forms of knowledge are embraced because they matter and are valued by those who are leading and who are affected by the approach.

This has implications for how we conceive 'knowledge'. Those who favour a 'knowledge transfer model' may believe that knowledge is something that can be packaged up and moved from one place to another, holding the belief that there is one 'answer' that exists and can be known by everyone. Others who advocate a 'translation model' assume that there are a range of ways that improved outcomes can be achieved and that these will be different for different people in different settings (Wieringa and Greenhalgh, 2015). This latter viewpoint emphasises the need for collaboration to understand diverse perspectives and is a better fit with asset-based approaches as it assumes that knowledge is constructed through a 'dynamic interchange' between a range of people and ideas. In practice, this highlights the importance of collectively learning by doing and reflecting together, rather than waiting for clear evidence about what works before trying anything new, which represents and values a form of 'practice-based evidence' (Allen and Glasby, 2010) reflected in asset-based methodologies.

Practice-based evidence is where 'research directly derives from practice concerns and is aimed at providing practice improvement' (Marsh and Fisher, 2010, p. 2). In other words it allows for complexity because it is grounded in the 'real' world, and practice is documented as it happens. It is an approach that furthers the argument that:

> the lived experience of service users or carers and the practice wisdom of practitioners can be just as valid a way of understanding the world as formal research (and possibly more valid for some questions) (Glasby, 2011, p. 89).

This thinking resonates with the assertions in the following quote from a policymaker:

> 'We are trying to gather evidence ourselves and we know that others are too. So, it's about trying to share knowledge and make sure that we share an understanding. I think as we go along, its building up the stories, building up the data, but not being afraid to act.' [policymaker]

As discussed earlier, this directly challenges much of the dominant discourse around evidence, which favours empirical research to drive decision-making where systematic reviews and RCTs are classified as the 'gold standard' of provision situated at the top of the evidence hierarchy, while case studies and professional experience are closer to the bottom (Cairney, 2015). This is a complex debate, but as Glasby and Beresford (2006, p. 281) highlight '… some research questions, proximity to the object being studied can be more appropriate than notions of "distance" and "objectivity"', suggesting a much more nuanced response to the hierarchy by recognising the importance of different forms of knowledge and ways of knowing in a variety of contexts.

Adopt a theory of change to understand connections and complexity

One of the reasons that asset-based approaches have received traction in recent years is their perceived ability to embrace the significant interconnectivity and complexity of life (Foot, 2012). This holistic quality means actively embracing and focusing on the dynamism and interaction between variables in order to aid understanding about how they link together, and the related impact of this connection. For example, although the well-being of an individual or a group of people within a community may be maintained or improved, it is difficult to prove that one approach over another brought about the change. Instead, from an asset-based perspective, the emphasis is on understanding how the connections between the range factors may have impacted. Thinking about the world in this way can uncover new possibilities and options not seen when variables are considered in isolation (Senge, 1990).

Theory of change

Asset-based approaches are focused on the relationships and connections between different variables, not the factors that separate them. As such, models of evaluation that are concerned with identifying and isolating variables in order to determine 'attribution' directly contrast with an asset-based approach. Theory of change (ToC) evaluation provides an alternative, where all partners and stakeholders involved in or affected by an intervention work together to establish the sequence of activities and outcomes required to bring about long-term change, as well as factors from the context which may influence this change. These are then mapped graphically, providing a representation of the 'pathway for change', or logic model. As Weiss (2001, p. 103) puts it:

> [ToC] brings to the surface the underlying assumptions about why a programme will work. It then tracks those assumptions through the collection and analysis of data at a series of stages along the way to final outcomes. The evaluation then follows each step to see whether the events assumed to take place in the programme actually do take place.

It is proposed that ToC methodologies are particularly suitable for asset-based approaches given the iterative and participative nature of their processes. Hopkins and Rippon (2015) suggest that ToC towards asset-based practice has four key stages, which are not linear and can be undertaken according to the context of the initiative:

- reframing towards assets;
- recognising assets;
- mobilising assets;
- co-producing assets and outcomes

Contribution analysis (CA) is one member of the ToC 'family' that seeks to uncover the contribution an intervention is making to observed outcomes. It specifically does not attempt to 'prove' that an intervention caused outcomes to be achieved. Instead CA provides an increased understanding of why the observed results have or have not occurred, creating a 'credible picture' of the role an intervention plays alongside other factors (Mayne, 2001). Adopting this type of framework for evaluation enables those who are involved to develop a ToC collaboratively and to discuss openly and debate the process and progress throughout its duration (Wimbush *et al.*, 2012).

The adoption of CA remains limited and as such the evidence with regards to its effectiveness in evaluating approaches (such as asset-based approaches) is slowly emerging. In a recent social services example, Stocks-Rankin (2015) suggests that, when using CA to understand complexity, there is a need to pay as much attention to the context as to the process of the work. As such, every attempt should be made to understand the system before and after the adoption of the approach so that any potential wider contextual or cultural changes can be documented. It follows that those who are using ToC approaches need to be careful to ensure that data collection can reflect these wider system changes.

Focus on the outcomes of participation

There has been an historic focus on performance metrics in the NHS and in local government, which focus on aspects of inputs, processes and outputs with much less attention paid to the ultimate outcomes of care as measured by quality of life: for example, by the reliance on HEAT targets (which quantify: Health improvement; Efficiency and governance; Access to service; and Treatment appropriate to individuals) as indicators of success. This focus on performance management, rather than outcomes, can lead to a tendency to concentrate on measuring what is convenient and available, rather than what will actually tell us whether we are achieving what is needed and wanted by those supported by services, their families and communities (Propper and Wilson, 2003).

The generation and collation of outcomes data measuring positive health and well-being can therefore be considered as a mechanism to balance out the traditional mortality, morbidity and condition-specific statistics that describe individuals in deficit terms (Foot, 2012). As such, for any organisation engaged in activities to pursue health and well-being, the focus on outcomes can be seen as a welcome step towards gaining a clearer understanding of the difference and contribution their activities make. However, in the context of co-production, Durose *et al.* (2014, p. 5) suggest that approaches that have relationship building at their heart can often sit 'awkwardly' alongside the need to be measurable for outcomes due to difficulties in 'capturing the emotional and transformative aspects' of the approach. Therefore approaches to measurement that include relational aspects may be useful for understanding the impact of asset-based approaches.

Researchers such as Fischbacher *et al.* (2013) indicate a step towards this through the proposal to focus on assessing the level of participation that is achieved and the extent to which the approach builds on individual and community strengths (empowerment). The question then becomes 'are asset-based approaches more participatory than other approaches?' and 'to what extent do asset-based approaches differ from other approaches in achieving these benefits?'. Here the crucial point is to be clear about whether participation (both in terms of the quality and impact of the participation) is an ambition in itself or a means to achieve positive outcomes for people and communities. It is necessary to make explicit and systematise the link between the process (involvement/participation) and the anticipated outcome so it is clear why participation is a major component in the adoption of the approach, and what has been achieved.

Accept that this work takes time
Hopkins and Rippon (2015, p. 23) suggest that 'an essential feature of "reframing" in the context of asset-based approaches for health is to move away from disease, illness- or deficit-defined targets to longer-term outcomes'. Therefore, with the person-centred/community-led, long-term and open-ended nature of asset-based approaches in mind, it is clear that measurement practices that assume that change should be recognisable after a fixed period of time are not aligned with the approach. Questioning the length of time until outcomes are met suggests that there is a predetermined end point somewhere down the line, which is a traditional conceptualisation that is unlikely to be able to accommodate the flexibility and uncertainty that are hallmarks of asset-based work. Instead it is necessary to see measurement and evaluation as integral to asset-based approaches; they are not disconnected from practice and planning.

Methods for identifying and mobilising assets
It has been contended that the use of established participatory outcomes-focused planning and evaluation approaches are most appropriate and effective for evaluation of asset-based approaches (GCPH, 2012). As such, this section will highlight a range of pragmatic tools and techniques to support policymakers, researchers

and practitioners working together with people and communities to identify assets and assess the benefits of asset-based approaches in practice at the individual, community and population level.

At the level of the individual

A number of tools are available to measure outcomes-focused, strengths-based approaches at the individual level. For these, it is important to distinguish between approaches that seek to understand expressed outcomes of people, and those that aim to measure 'wellbeing' as there will be relevant implications for the processes of measurement that are adopted (Barrie and Miller, 2015). Given that relationships are the cornerstone of asset-based approaches, it is considered that flexible, conversational approaches (such as Talking Points as described in Figure 4.1) can provide more effective ways of helping practitioners and those supported by services to understand collaboratively and measure a person's journey towards their desired outcomes, and the associated link to their well-being. This can provide a means to improve the person's experience of care and support as well as producing data to prompt service improvements and decision-making (Cook and Miller, 2012).

Figure 4.1: CASE STUDY – Talking points.

Talking Points is an evidence-based organisational approach that puts people using services and unpaid carers at the centre of the support they receive. It is a conversational approach, which involves working with the supported person and their carers to identify what is important to them or what they want to achieve, and then working backwards to identify how to get there.

Adoption of the approach means:

- engaging with the person to identify and plan how everyone is going to work together to achieve outcomes;
- recording the outcomes in a support plan, which is shared and which can be used to check whether outcomes have been achieved or if the plan needs to change;
- using the information to ensure what matters to people influences planning, commissioning and service improvement.

Benefits of adopting the Talking Points approach include:

- improving outcomes and preventing deterioration by providing an opportunity for the person to contribute to their care;

○ enabling the organisation to move away from a service-led approach to one that draws on the strengths and capacities of those who are being supported;

○ supporting the organisation to deliver on policy goals including increased independence, personalisation, enablement, prevention, improved integration and a shift in the balance of care from hospital to the community;

○ reorientation of systems and process to support new ways of working and engagement of people across the organisation.

Source: Cook and Miller, 2012.

Storytelling is another example of a flexible, informal and appreciative way of collecting information about people's own experiences of successful projects or activities, their own skills and achievements and what they hope for (Foot and Hopkins, 2010). The process of telling tales can benefit the storyteller as it 'empower(s), encourage(s) personal growth and build(s) resilience' and has also been found to enhance relationships between the teller and the listener (Drumm, 2013, p. 2).

Researchers have highlighted that subjective measures and personal stories 'can be powerful illustrations of change and can indicate the success of asset-based approaches' (Hopkins and Rippon, 2015, p. 46). Stories, as illustrated in the quote below from a community development manager, have been referred to as 'data with soul' and are a form of evidence that can provide rich qualitative data to support and be considered alongside statistical and quantitative data to provide a more rounded account of the impact of the asset-based approach in practice (Foot, 2012). As such, the use of storytelling can also be a powerful vehicle for understanding and communicating the ways in which assets and asset-based programmes affect health and well-being.

> 'Story is a huge element of what we do and so we start off by telling people a bit about our story as an organisation … but also pointing out that there are a lot of people involved along the years that have helped write that story, and you are part of the next chapter, and we are part of your story.' [community development manager]

At the community level

There are a variety of measurement tools that have traditionally been employed to support and evaluate community development approaches. For example, frameworks such as Achieving Better Community Development (Barr and Hashagen, 2000), LEAP (Learning, Evaluation And Planning) for Health (SCDC, 2003) and the Well-being And Resilience Measure (WARM) (Health Foundation, 2011; Mguni and Bacon, 2010) are participatory, outcomes-focused and acknowledge complexity at the level of the community. As well as seeking greater understanding, these types of methods seek to bring about change in and of themselves. For example, it is argued that engagement in the design and process of collaborative evaluation is empowering and transforming as it allows people 'to develop new ways of thinking, behaving and practicing' (Hills and Mullett, 2000).

The LEAP for Health framework (see Figure 4.2) is a model of community development and change that focuses on process – how workers involved in community development activity can promote individual and community empowerment and capacity by adopting a planned and participatory approach to practice. A strength of the LEAP approach is that it promotes making the best use of limited resources by bringing together all key stakeholders including those supported by services to see what can be done (Dailly and Barr, 2008).

Figure 4.2: The five steps of the LEAP for Health framework.

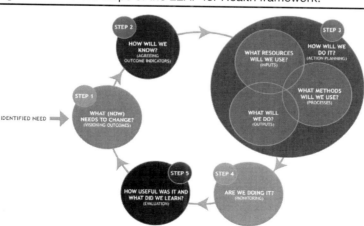

There is a strong similarity between the values and principles that underpin an asset-based approach and participatory action research. For example, they are both appreciative in that they recognise strengths and assets as a starting point for enquiry and build and embed resilience and capacity through the process of research itself. This is noted in this summary of good practice principles (sourced from Sharp, 2012) where it is stated that:

○ work should be rooted in the context where those who are involved determine what is important;

○ the focus becomes testing and refining outcomes;

○ those who are involved determine the values and purpose of the research process, including the success criteria that will judge the outcome of the research;

○ it is appreciative in nature and recognises strengths as a starting point for inquiry;

○ collaboration is at its heart, is inclusive of all kinds of knowing and recognises the importance of sharing knowledge;

○ meaning and interpretation evolves as the work is undertaken;

○ the focus of the work can adapt as necessary and there is openness to new information;

○ it happens in real time and there is continual learning and reflection built into the process.

Researchers suggest that the appreciative element is useful for supporting the development of asset-centric practice (Foot and Hopkins, 2010) because when we pay attention, are curious and cherish what is working well it can inspire change and improvement (Hornstrup and Johansen, 2009). Appreciative inquiry (AI), for example, is a process for valuing and drawing out the strengths and successes in the history of a group, community or organisation and has been described as a 'relational process that focuses on creative conversations between people, and where the outcome is co-created' (Dewar and Sharp, 2013, p. 3).

At population level
There have been attempts at a national level in Scotland to improve outcomes at scale through the use of improvement methodologies. Indeed the move towards a Scottish Approach to Government, as

highlighted in Chapters 1 and 3, is underpinned by improvement methodology. According to the Health Foundation (2011, p. 6):

> Improvement science focuses on systematically and rigorously exploring 'what works' to improve quality in healthcare and the best ways to measure and disseminate this [is] to ensure positive change.

Improvement methodology is therefore the framework for the delivery of large-scale change across systems, and not just the process of improvement.

Although these methods have been successful in clinical settings – for example, in reducing hospital-acquired infections (Nicolay *et al.*, 2011) – there is some debate about the appropriateness of using improvement methods to support evidence gathering on the impact of asset-based approaches at a community level (Barr, 2014). For example, in order to understand whether improvement methodologies are aligned with asset-based approaches, it is crucial to determine: who defines the issues that are seen as in need of attention?; who identifies the hypotheses that are considered worthy of testing; and who determines the basis on which the evidence constitutes improvement? If these decisions are made externally from the person or community in question, then it may suggest that the person or the community is the target of the intervention, rather than a co-designer of the ways things are done. Given that the principle importance of asset-based approaches is the empowerment of individuals and local communities by placing them centrally in design, planning, delivery and crucially, the evaluation of the services and supports they use, this would seem at odds with the underpinning theory of asset-based approaches.

Similarly, in terms of the small experimental cycles of Plan Do Study Act (PDSA), the focus on 'test conditions' may contrast with the principles of asset-based approaches, which are rooted in context. At a community level, it is often the process of action involved in testing the hypotheses that lead to very different understandings of the context and value of the intervention, and as such it could be misleading to attribute success or failure of improvement without a clearer understanding of the relationship between the approach and the wider context (Barr, 2014). Similarly the focus on isolating singular variables to test sits uneasily with asset-based approaches, where the focus is more understanding connections between variables and where it is not possible to fix and identify variables in advance.

Finally the focus on determining 'what works' also potentially conflicts with an asset-based approach. While it is important to recognise and value what we know from empirical and practice-based evidence, tensions may emerge at experimentation stage when adapting the approaches to context, as asset-based proponents equally value local knowledge and place importance on local ownership of that know-how. However others suggest that improvement methodologies and asset-based approaches such as co-production are not mutually exclusive (Maher, 2015), and it is important not to over-simplify these debates. Indeed, if the model of improvement is undertaken with an attitude of AI in collaboration with people and communities it may in fact be complementary.

The range of tools and processes for evaluating asset-based approaches should not be considered a tick-box exercise to be routinely completed by practitioners; it is crucial that the underpinning values of appreciation, participation and shared implementation are understood and embraced in order to support the wider cultural shift towards promoting the strengths of individuals and communities. What matters is ensuring that the methods, the intervention and the purpose of evaluation are appropriately matched (Coote *et al.*, 2004). A more valuable focus in the context of asset-based approaches may be to promote responsiveness and sensitivity to local contexts and the learning needs of those who are involved (Hopkins and Rippon, 2015).

Conclusion

There is an old Scottish proverb that states: 'You don't make sheep any fatter by weighing them'. This seems neatly to summarise the challenges of measurement that this chapter has attempted to present and discuss. The conversation regarding the measurement of asset-based approaches is alive in Scotland and a number of key questions remain: for example, how can we ensure that we measure in an asset-based way?; are we striving to understand the approach itself, or the outcomes of the approach?; and how can we better compare an asset-based approach with other ways of working?

What is clear is that outcomes in and of themselves are difficult to measure. There is no perfect measure; what is important is that the choice of method is appropriate, acceptable to those involved and fits with what the person or group is trying to achieve (Barrie and Miller, 2015). Some consider that evaluation in the context of asset-based approaches should be conceived of as reflective practice, and that learning should be part of and integral to the evolution of the approach in practice (GCPH, 2012). The narrative in this chapter offers ways in which the research for asset-based approaches can be strengthened, such as by embracing the interrelated nature of action, reflection and evaluation, adopting a ToC, focusing on the outcomes of participation and taking a longer-term view.

In the next chapter we consider what we need to do to make asset-based approaches happen and explore a number of the enabling conditions and foundations that are required for them to develop and be adopted in practice.

PART 3

The Reality of Asset-Based Approaches

CHAPTER 5

Creating the Conditions: What helps?

Introduction

Asset-based approaches are happening in many different contexts and settings in Scotland and the across the UK (McLean and McNeice, 2012; Hopkins and Rippon, 2015), but they 'do not just happen', nor are they a DIY approach to improving health and well-being. As discussed in Chapter 1, a healthy participatory democracy is a fundamental pre-condition for an asset-based approach to embed at structural level. That said, there are important roles for the NHS, local government and the third sector, community organisations and their partners in creating safe and supportive places, fostering resilience and enabling individuals and communities to take more control of their health and lives.

However, before discussing the conditions that support and enable this way of working, it is important to remember (as discussed in detail in Chapter 3) that a key feature of asset-based working is valuing the skills and knowledge and connections in individuals and communities. Asset-based activities, whether within communities or services, are united by how they go about their business, in what they are trying to achieve, how they engage with people, and the relationships that they build.

Throughout the chapter quotes are again used from our interviewees to illustrate and reinforce key points from a range of perspectives and from practice. The chapter also presents a case study of a service working with young people and examples of current initiatives seeking to develop collaborative leadership and workforce skills and knowledge around asset-based approaches.

So what foundations need to be in place for asset-based approaches to develop, grow and thrive? From our own interviews, it was clear that both internal and external factors are important, and in this chapter we consider some of the conditions that can enable and support asset-based working with individuals, in communities and in services. As one of the community-based project managers observed:

'I think the environment counts for a lot as far as whether people are equipped to tap into their assets or their inner resources.' [community-based project manager]

What needs to be in place to support and enable asset-based approaches in practice?

The full 'business case' for asset-based approaches in a UK health context is still being developed (Hopkins and Rippon, 2015). When exploring the enabling foundations and conditions required for asset-based working within existing services and areas of innovative practice, a number of requirements and levers for change are evident. These are discussed in turn below and include:

- ❍ a receptive policy landscape;
- ❍ a healthy organisational culture;
- ❍ collective leadership and shared responsibilities;
- ❍ relationships;
- ❍ skills and resources.

A receptive policy landscape

Discussion in Chapters 1 and 2 showed that, in recent years, policy in Scotland has shifted emphasis towards prevention and the need to work differently to tackle persistent inequalities. As a result the language of asset-based approaches now permeates much of the health and social services policy literature. The trend towards considering, developing and delivering new and innovative ways of working was already underway prior to the fiscal crisis of 2008, where the benefits of working in ways in which people are more involved in determining their own health outcomes were becoming better understood (Christie, 2011). However the scale of the recession has been an important stimulant for a more pressing and fundamental rethink on the role of local government and public services, and how and where services are delivered.

The changing role of public services crosses conventional political and organisational lines (Elvidge, 2014); policymakers and politicians are now taking an explicit interest in 'bottom up' ways of working that give people and communities more control. This includes the range of different ways and locations in which health and social services can be provided and any changes to the role of professionals.

Creating an enabling and receptive environment for change is not an easy task for government, but Scotland has at present a strong core narrative, which puts community and social relations at the heart of developing health and social policy (Scottish Government, 2010b; 2011b; Scottish Parliament, 2015a). As highlighted in Chapters 1 and 2, asset-based approaches and the values and principles of this way of working now cut across a range of policy areas and legislative frameworks, raising awareness of this way of working and supporting a shift of practice in this direction. This creates an enabling foundation for making asset-based working happen, now and in the longer term.

A healthy organisational culture

Reference to 'culture' is a common feature of the discussion about the implementation of asset-based working and the value of operating differently within public services, reflecting the importance placed on the need for a sense of shared values and beliefs (Drumm, 2012). A key feature of organisations that are set up to enable change, in an asset-based way, is the support of the collective and collaborative efforts of individuals, communities and different partner organisations in the design and delivery of services.

The importance of developing, fostering and embedding a positive, healthy and shared culture is acknowledged as a key priority within the agenda for the integration of health and social services in Scotland. This acknowledges that seeking to retain existing cultures when bringing organisations together may lead to a struggle for dominance and a concern that the culture of one or other of the partners in the collaboration will win (Petch, 2013). The recognition of the need to focus on the six key dimensions of concentrating on outcomes, vision, leadership, culture, local context and time required for a new cultural identity is an imperative for the success of the integrated care process. A joined-up and preventative approach to service delivery is a key feature of an asset-driven, enabling system.

A 'healthy' culture is amenable to and supportive of change – it harnesses the commitment of staff to valuing and building the strengths, skills and aspirations of individuals and communities, and is one in which staff feel valued as assets themselves. To create this shift, staff must also be engaged in the change process and understand their role in delivering successful services. This means co-produced organisational values, a positive and supported attitude to risk-taking, and the active engagement with the individuals they work, support and engage with (Allcock *et al.*, 2015). The importance of remaining true to personal values and organisational culture, paying attention to underpinning relationships and practice is highlighted in the quotes below from our interviews with managers and practitioners across health and community services. This shift is creating a challenging new relationship between individuals, communities and the service providers:

> 'It's the culture you create and the extent to which it mirrors the change you are trying to bring about in the world.' [community-based project manager]

> 'It's about personal values as well as the values of your agency.' [community development manager]

> 'I think it has had a positive impact on me, as an individual – I think I am more confident in my role, and I think I am hoping that what I do here … the way that it's enhanced me, I hope then is a benefit to everything else, the services around me, the people that use our services, by the way that I approach things, view things.' [health practitioner]

An enabling environment supports strong relationships in and between staff and organisations, and encourages openness and permission from organisational leads, national bodies and politicians to take risks and learn from mistakes. This helps to create a learning organisation, where policies locally and nationally help rather than hinder creativity, innovation and new ways of working (Allcock *et al.*, 2015). The importance of this type of enabling condition is also recognised at the level of policy development and is further illustrated by a quote from a national policymaker:

'You need a very permissive, open system, which allows
people to try new things, and share openly with others, the
things that work and the things that haven't.' [policymaker]

The combined efforts of people in their own communities offer-
ing help and support to one another, supported by an enabling
health and social services infrastructure, offers a new frame of
reference for health systems (Hopkins and Rippon, 2015). This has
the potential to support transformation at system level through the
development of a more equal relationship between services and
the people who are supported by them. In a healthy organisational
culture, work to build health-enhancing assets, organisations and
services must not only focus on psychosocial assets such as skills,
confidence and self-esteem but must also recognise the social, cultural, physical and environmental factors that influence inequalities in health and well-being. A healthy culture must be able to
understand and work within the wider influences on health, such
as housing, education and employment.

Collective leadership and shared responsibilities

For asset-based approaches to be successful – whether within
projects, services or systems – facilitative leadership in its many
guises is a fundamental component. Asset-based ways of working
emphasise the importance of the collective and distributed nature
of leadership as illustrated in the quote below from a manager of
a service for young people facilitating collaboration and sparking
enthusiasm (West *et al.*, 2014):

'Everybody in this organisation is in a leadership position,
because everyone can ask the question, 'how can I improve
what I am doing to meet our purpose of helping [client
group] … or how can I help my colleagues meet our purpose? It doesn't matter what position you are in – if you are
working in this way then you are demonstrating leadership.'
[NGO manager]

Leadership happens at all levels, it is not always from the front
or from the top, but often through facilitative roles within organisations and communities, with the act of leading being about

knowing when to step back and let others take ownership. Leadership is about how a person behaves and what they do. The ability to engage people with a clear vision for change and the need to work differently, with a renewed focus centred on supporting people for positive outcomes and improved life chances, is arguably the most important factor in a shift towards asset-based working (Allcock *et al.*, 2015). Committed, respected leadership that engages people, staff and other organisations is a requirement for success, in whatever field. To support the reality and value of this way of working, leaders and managers should be able to: inspire, influence and advocate asset-based approaches; 'convince the unconvinced'; drive and respond to the required fundamental changes in power-sharing; and exemplify the principles themselves in the positive way in which they work with others. An example of a practical leadership programme set up to test and enable collaborative leadership within the public sector is provided in Figure 5.1.

Figure 5.1: Workforce Scotland's Enabling Collaborative Leadership – Pioneer Programme.

Within public service there is the clear expectation that staff work in partnership with others – with staff in other organisations and with the people that use services. Change is a constant feature and, in the midst of the pressures of delivery, well-intentioned efforts to take time for learning can too easily evaporate. The Pioneer Programme aims to find simple ways to learn from and with others. The focus of the programme is on exploring and developing the core knowledge, skills, behaviours and approaches that support the development of collaborative leadership. Using an action-research approach, participants experience the practical benefits of working collaboratively and have an explicit role in demonstrating and supporting the development of collaborative working in their own organisations, drawing on a systematic approach to inquiry, multiple perspectives, testing out new ways of acting and learning from experience.

Further information can be found at: https://workforcescotland.wordpress.com/ecl (accessed 11 January 2016)

Values-driven leadership will win hearts and minds on the frontline but they also need to build capability in quality improvement and innovation. Effective leaders, at whatever level, challenge the status quo and are open to new ideas and agendas, but they must be supported within their role if this innovation is to continue (South *et al.*, 2013). Embedding asset-based working cannot therefore be reliant on or be the vision of one person; it must be rooted within the organisational culture and ethos. Key to embedding these ideas in mainstream practice across all parts of the system are leadership and knowledge sharing, transfer and translation. This was acknowledged in an interview with a community development manager:

> 'The sharing of knowledge and experience across the sectors is key.' [community development manager]

In further supporting the implementation of asset-based approaches, leaders must champion this way of working (Hopkins and Rippon, 2015), locally through integrated partnership boards, local government, local health boards and community planning partnerships, and nationally across the UK by influencing and engaging in dialogue with the Scottish government, NHS Scotland and Public Health England. However it must be acknowledged not only that managers are tasked to provide leadership, direction and inspiration, but that it is also vital that they have effective operational management of programmes and services to improve health and well-being through robust processes, governance and accountability, achievable expectations and a focus on delivery (Allcock *et al.*, 2015).

Driving forward asset-based approaches are the responsibility of all of us. All parts of society have a role in improving the well-being of citizens and communities (Wallace, 2013). This requires effective partnerships between individuals, communities, the public, the private sector and the state; however sharing these responsibilities can be challenging and the building of effective partnerships and shared interests and direction takes time.

Partnerships are crucial across all levels, within and between organisations, and between the state and communities and individuals. Asset-based approaches promote and are successful when there is a shared responsibility for complex social issues and where it is recognised that these issues are not the responsibility of a single organisation or sector. Instead the key priority is individual and community well-being rather than organisational targets (Brotchie, 2013), and the focus is on providing joined-up and preventative approaches to service delivery. This change in focus for services and organisations, on outcomes rather than targets, requires to be supported by appropriate physical and financial resources, which enable the drive towards preventative action (rather than crisis management) and joined-up working across systems and sectors (Wallace, 2013).

Relationships

Relationships, interactions, dialogue and connecting are all central features of asset-based practice (Hopkins and Rippon, 2015), the importance of which cannot be overstated (GCPH and SCDC, 2015a). In building successful relationships, a combination of good personal qualities and strong professional attributes is essential. Cultivating these personal relationships with others, in the community and within and between organisations, requires a willingness to invest time, energy and self without guarantee of a beneficial return. Relationships imply a connection between individuals, whether that is in relation to family, community, working life, friendship groups or a shared interest or affinity. It is accepted that it is the quality of these relationships, rather than the quantity, that is important for health and mental well-being (Diener and Seligman, 2002), as illustrated in Figure 5.2. Positive and supportive relationships can give rise to feelings of optimism, confidence, empowerment, a sense of hope and a possibility about ourselves, others and the world around us, and where openness and sense of confidence can lead to other positive experiences.

Figure 5.2: Case study – Includem.

Includem is a specialist charity established in 2000 with the sole focus of delivering support to the most vulnerable and challenging young people in society. The flexible and responsive, one-to-one support provided by Includem at the time of need helps young people, parents and carers make positive changes to their attitude, behaviours and relationships, twenty-four hours a day, every single day of the year.

For some young people, life is a series of problems. They often feel completely alone, and cannot see any future at all. At Includem they stick with each young person, helping them realise they can change their circumstances, and helping them build a better life. No matter how tough their circumstances, they always start from a point of view of valuing them, engaging with them, building one-to-one trusting relationships – and refusing to give up.

> '... ultimately it is about the relationships – the quality of those relationships, if you don't have the quality of the relationship it doesn't matter what methods and techniques you have or use – you need people who are able to form relationships with genuine warmth.' [service manager]

There are five values at the heart of everything Includem does. These are:

○ the belief that no young person is beyond help;
○ that a flexible, quality service is guaranteed;
○ the aim to rebuild family relationships;
○ the provision of value for money;
○ that young people have the best chance of a successful adulthood.

> 'The approach we take has to be about getting alongside [young people], accepting them as the whole people they are, believing in them, having hope for them when they don't have hope for themselves, and working with them to help them find a different vision for themselves ... finding the parts of themselves that will include some natural assets and strengths, but it may mean the need to develop assets if they are going to move on ... like all of us, they need to believe that learning is possible.' [service manager]

Includem is anchored in an understanding of the importance of relationships and social networks in the creation and maintenance of life chances and health. Includem's services are rooted in evidence-based practice and shaped to reflect current research about effective ways of helping young people achieve a better life. Since inception, Includem has been committed to rigorous monitoring and evaluation of services and the impact they have on young people.

Further information can be found at: http://www.includem.org (accessed 11 January 2016).

___

Skills and resources
Workforce development

Moving asset-based approaches from the margins to the mainstream has far-reaching implications for organisations and the staff who work in them, for roles and skills, and for workforce composition and regulation. This means a fundamental shift in practice for a range of professionals, which expands beyond traditional health and social services roles and is one that will require considerable investment in the key workforce for public health and social services.

At the level of the workforce, the quality of the relationships and interactions between people has a profound effect on practitioners' health and well-being and satisfaction with work. Research with healthcare staff has demonstrated that positive interactions with, and social support from, colleagues is associated with increased job satisfaction (Adams and Bond, 2000), reduced stress (Coffey and Coleman, 2001; Payne, 2001) and lower absence from work due to ill health (Kivimaki *et al.*, 2000).

Staff responsibilities will change as support services are developed and redirected towards asset-based principles. Frontline staff and their managers must be equipped, and confident, to work in new and different ways. To support asset-based working, staff will have a focus on brokering, facilitation and enabling rather than on delivering, where active listening, power-sharing, collaboration and networking are key skills in encouraging communities and individuals, with support, do things for themselves (Hopkins and Rippon, 2015). This was reiterated by one of the community development managers interviewed for this book:

'There are some really basic values and attitudes like working with people in ways that consistently view people as active participants and not passive recipients of services.'
[community development manager]

New deeper relationships with individuals and communities must be built so that citizens and service users can be properly engaged in the design, delivery and development of services (Brotchie, 2013), with a focus on recognising the importance of responding flexibly to local circumstances and local priorities. These skills and personal attributes, and the types of relationships they create, are in contrast to the transactional and standardised relationships between professionals, clients and patients that have become typical of health and social services (Hopkins and Rippon, 2015).

Following recommendations from the Christie Commission (Christie, 2011) the Skilled Workers, Skilled Citizens initiative (see

Figure 5.3), sponsored by the Scottish government and the Scottish Leaders' Forum, was established to explore, in detail, the skills and knowledge required by the public sector workforce to embed and extend asset-based values and principles across organisations.

Figure 5.3: Skilled workers skilled citizens.

This is a national initiative that is gathering evidence and sharing experience and learning based on practical examples of asset-based approaches in action. Its focus is to bring together many different public service organisations that are engaging with the people who use their services; and to help develop and train the workforce to deliver better services.

The initiative is currently engaging with a wide range of staff and organisations from public service organisations from across Scotland to come to an agreed and shared understanding of the skills and knowledge they need to embed and deliver asset-based working, establish a number of pioneer sites to explore and illustrate asset-based working across the public sector, and to develop a range of practical tools and resources to support staff and organisations working in this way.

Further information can be found at: http://www.scottishleadersforum.org/ skilled-workers-skilled-citizen (accessed 11 January 2016)

Funding and resources

As discussed in Chapter 1, neoliberal policies with a focus on the market have led to large inequalities in the distribution of wealth. In a more enabling state, with a focus on tackling inequalities and improving outcomes, a major challenge is to ensure that financial investment is distributed fairly – to those that would benefit the most. This is a particular challenge when supporting community grassroots activities (Brotchie, 2013), which are often fragile when resources are tight and which may not link directly to local or national targets and preventative action. Much of the asset-based working that takes place within communities and services at present relies to some extent on the availability of financial support from dedicated funding organisations and from local or national government or health boards, which is often provided for a limited and short period of time. The nature of the current funding environment is highlighted in the quote below from a community-based project manager:

'I think there is a very powerful culture of being seen not to fail, and I think that the funding climate we work in creates that. I know a lot of funders have started to ask, "what were your unintended outcomes, and what was the learning", and they are starting to encourage people to be more honest. But ultimately I don't think it goes far enough.'
[community-based project manager]

To support asset-based work, the NHS and local authorities will be required to prioritise investment to communities and community-based projects to support them to mobilise their own local assets, which are often more immediately responsive to local need. This is especially important during times of reductions in public services and the impact this may have on widening inequalities (Hopkins and Rippon, 2015).

Alongside funding and the allocation of resources, practical support, training, skills and knowledge at community level also matter. Communities and community organisations often call for advice on good governance, accounting and financial management, guidance and signposting to support sources, access to tools and resources, mentoring support and help with connecting and networking. This is often described as community capacity building (see Chapter 2 for further detail).

Funding support and resources need to be allocated over a sufficient period of time to increase the likelihood of success and demonstration of outcomes in the longer term, and be more flexible in nature to support development and longer-term ambitions. Funders, commissioners and organisations must be 'in it for the long game'. This is discussed in more detail below.

Time

If services are to be re-envisaged in an enabling way with a focus on assets and strengths transformed, rather than simply tinkered with, then it is crucial that a sufficient period of time and resources are set aside. It is important not to rush new approaches through in a top-down fashion, due to the restricted availability of funding or political timing, and to allow service users, local residents and stakeholders time to be properly involved in the design and developmental stages. This shift in focus, ethos and activity does not happen overnight, as demonstrated by a number of research studies exploring asset-based working in a range of settings (McLean and McNeice, 2012; Brotchie, 2013; GCPH and SCDC, 2015b). It can take many months or years to build trust and bring together communities, different services and systems to work in a different way in partnership with a common purpose. It is also well recognised that sustained energy and effort are needed for communities to organise, to identify a shared interest or priority, to establish relationships and networks between people, between people and organisations and local services, and to build local capacity for action. As discussed earlier, time is also a crucial factor in the development of relationships where the provision of dedicated time and space for positive conversations supports the fostering of new collaborations, new connections and new networks, helping to identify new possibilities, at local and national levels, thereby building capacity for collective action.

Development of the evidence base

Finally, in supporting and creating the conditions above and in continuing to make the case for asset-based approaches, the further development of the recognised evidence base plays a crucial role. Although there is a developing body of evidence on the benefits of community participation and empowerment in addressing the social determinants of health (Marmot, 2010) and although they are interrelated, the evidence base for the impact of asset-based approaches remains limited and uncertain to date and inevitably gaps exist (as described in detail in Chapter 4) (Sigerson and Gruer; 2011; Baker, 2014; A. Morgan, 2014).

The dynamic nature of participatory and asset-based work is not always reflected in the academic literature. Many successful community-based projects and small tests of change happen out with the radar of formal and informal evaluations, and the effects often occur long after researchers and evaluators have left (Savage *et al.*, 2009; South, 2015). As discussed in Chapter 4, the continued growth and changing nature of the evidence base, incorporating the many different forms of research, data, knowledge and experience, is important in supporting community practitioners and local organisations when 'making the case' for asset-based activity and when convincing policymakers and commissioners that investment in this way of working will have a lasting impact on reducing health inequalities and will lead to better outcomes.

Conclusion

Across research, learning and practice a number of core factors appear to be important in creating the right kind of 'enabling' conditions for the development of asset-based approaches. This chapter has touched on a number of these conditions, but there are indeed many more. If we are serious about 'making it happen', then we need to consider what is required, what works and to what extent, in individuals, communities and organisations, and what more we should bring to the table to create the conditions for this approach to succeed and flourish.

The chapter has reflected on the importance of a receptive policy landscape and the importance of time in supporting a systems-level shift towards a different way of working. We have touched on the importance of a shared ethos and culture about what it means to be 'healthy' and the key role of leadership in inspiring and advocating change. We have discussed the benefits of building new, more equal relationships between services and communities – a theme that runs throughout this book. This chapter has highlighted the need for skills development of the existing and new workforce, and the importance of investment in communities as key actors for change.

In the next chapter we consider and discuss the opposite side of this debate, the challenges that exist from moving this approach from the margins to being a core part of the mainstream, and discuss why disconnect exists between aspiration, uptake and implementation.

CHAPTER 6

Key Challenges: What is stopping us?

Introduction

Despite the prominence of asset-based approaches in policy as discussed in Chapter 1, and the emergence of pockets of related activity across Scotland as highlighted in case studies throughout this text, there remain significant challenges that hinder the adoption of the approach and the ability for it to be sustained in practice.

The first step in overcoming challenges is often to acknowledge that they exist. It is beyond the scope of this book to provide an exhaustive list of the many features that contribute to the gap between policy aspiration and the reality of implementation of asset-based approaches. Instead, the focus of this chapter is to provide an overview of key interrelated barriers in the hope that identifying these features will not detract or dissuade people from recognising the strengths of asset-based approaches, but will help explain the limited progress in moving the approach into the mainstream. We particularly focus on the themes of:

- ❏ inhibitive organisational cultures;
- ❏ mistrust;
- ❏ austerity;
- ❏ achieving scale.

The challenges of implementing an asset-based approach were particularly salient for our interviewees and as such quotes are used to provide contextual evidence from practice to reinforce key points. A case study is also provided to demonstrate how some of these challenges have been overcome.

What hinders the adoption of asset-based approaches in practice?

Inhibitive organisational cultures

Asset-based approaches are clearly aligned with the current policy direction, they are overtly referenced in legislation and guidance (see Chapter 1 for more details) and they are congruent with the values of community development, health and social services practice. However, as we have shown, they are not always supported by the structures and cultures in which practitioners operate. Researchers suggest that the transformational potential of asset-based approaches will not be realised unless new organisational cultures underpinned by the values of the approach are developed (Durose *et al.*, 2013, in the context of co-production) and that these values are applied equally to organisational change as well as practice change (S. Morgan, 2014).

Altering well-established cultures and associated systems is difficult. Duffy and Fulton (2010) argue that it is so complex that the tendency is to superimpose new approaches on top of old ones, leaving the old system intact beneath. This can result in competing layers of rules, audit processes and targets combining to make an inflexible, unwieldy system, which inhibits the capacity for new approaches to take root. These competing layers have been said to result in increased bureaucracy and hierarchy where standardised interventions determined from the top dominate (Seddon, 2008; Munro, 2004; Christiansen and Bunt, 2012; Arnaboldi *et al.*, 2015). This is a marked departure from the open, emergent and risk-enabling culture required to support asset-based approaches so they flourish, as described in the previous chapter and was acknowledged by many of our interviewees as highlighted below:

> 'There are obstacles to [the] successful application of strengths-based or asset-based approaches in Scotland. One of these is the normal institutional culture of institutions like health boards, local councils planning people etc. ... They tend to need things to be planned, they like to do things in terms of service providers and service recipients: it's like a customer relationship.' [community development manager]

Performance management systems, a focus on targets and all of the associated bureaucracy, as well as the imperative to make efficiencies in the public sector, can have a detrimental effect on practice resulting in practitioners strictly adhering to policy and processes rather than doing what is right for the person supported by their service (Munro, 2004; Miller, 2010). Some commentators have indeed observed that this has systematically reduced the 'human' in 'human services' (Graeber, 2015) and has limited the capacity for creativity, innovation and flexibility (Miller, 2010). For example, Andrews *et al.* (2009) found that 'service-led' models prevail with many staff focusing solely on addressing immediate needs, rather than recognising the 'little things' that can better support positive outcomes to be achieved. These combined layers have been said to contribute to a risk-averse system where practitioners are unsupported to try new approaches for fear that they will be reprimanded if mistakes are made – the counter to the learning culture highlighted in the previous chapter (Petts *et al.*, 2001). Indeed, social workers have been referred to as 'assessors of risk, at risk and as a risk' (McLaughlin, 2007, p. 1263), a detail that was pointedly made by some of our statutory sector interviewees:

> 'And certainly in the statutory services, I think we are less likely to take risks because people's ultimate fear is that you are going to get struck off, or there will be some kind of litigation.' [health practitioner]

Together this suggests that, although the incentive for staff to adopt asset-based practice may be clear from a policy perspective, the barriers existing within systems can combine to limit practitioner capacity to be able to work more flexibly and responsively alongside those supported by services (Seddon, 2008; Miller, 2010).

Lack of time and capacity to work directly with people

Adopting an asset-based approach is fundamentally about fostering trusting relationships, where direct contact between people and practitioners who have the time and incentive to interact flexibly with people to establish positive relationships is paramount (GCPH, 2014). It would therefore appear reasonable to suggest that, if practitioners are going to be enabled to change their practice, they have to be given space and time to think and practise differently (S. Morgan, 2014).

However, using child protection social work as an example, recent reports highlight that this field has become so bureaucratic and paper-laden that 80% of practitioners' time is spent form-filling rather than supporting people (Novell, 2014). Lack of time is commonly reported by home care workers (Cobban, 2004; Innes *et al.*, 2006), and the same is true for community development practitioners whose role has shifted from hands-on work in communities to staff managing 'an array of sessional staff working on part-time, low-paid and insecure contracts' (Emejulu, 2015, p. 4).

Furthermore, before the financial crisis became a reality, many local authorities in Scotland were already reducing their ability and capacity to engage with and support communities, with neighbour-hood community development work all but being eradicated and reductions in numbers of CLD practitioners because of budget repri-oritisation. A wide range of officers across local government and national agencies now have an element of responsibility for commu-nity development-related activity within their role, but this is often implicit rather than explicit and many lack experience or confidence in working in this way (Garven *et al.*, 2014).

As highlighted in Chapter 5, the importance of relationships in supporting positive outcomes for people is crucial. Therefore pres-sures on the capacity and lack of time of the workforce to build these positive relationships could be potentially very damaging, not only for the outcomes for people and communities but also for the job satisfaction of the workforce. Frontline workers identify job satisfac-tion as being centrally related to their contact with service users and the progress that is being made with them (Penna *et al.*, 1995), as well as the quality of support and supervision received (Carpenter *et al*, 2012). Indeed, there is some evidence indicating that practitioners relate to people supported by services in similar ways to how they are managed (Munro, 2010, West *et al*, 2014). With less time invested to build relationships, it could be considered that practitioners will be less able to provide appropriate choice and flexibility (Cobban, 2004; SCIE, 2010), and could become less fulfilled in their role.

Rigid roles

The move towards an asset-based approach 'changes the way authority is exercised', resulting in an increasing acknowledgement and emphasis placed on the value of personal experience, rather than on deference to expert opinion and knowledge (Griffiths et al., 2009, p. 92). Practitioners are the experts in their profession, and the people involved are the authority in their own lives, with the overall knowledge being shared and valued equally (SCIE, 2013). This requires a shift in organisational culture and roles from 'having all the answers' to realising that, in opening up discussions with individuals and communities, an opportunity is created for them to contribute (Boyle et al., 2010). In this way, as described in the previous chapter, there is an increased appetite to place trust in the workforce, to enable them to take initiative and to bring their 'whole selves' to work (Miller and Hall, 2013); for them to be people first, and professional second.

While there is little evidence of this shift being refuted in theory, in reality – instead of roles widening out to embrace asset-based approaches – there is some question over the time available for staff to reflect, share and shape practice, to develop relationships and to engage the communities where they work (Asquith et al., 2005; Seddon, 2008). Community development practitioners in our interviews highlighted this point:

> 'In other words, we want to have a plan. We want to have a framework. We want to feel in control of that and we see things in terms of services. There are people there who receive services and our job, statutory job is to somehow provide services.' [community development manager]

In the CLD workforce, the majority of practitioners now focus on youth work and adult learning, with a lower percentage directly involved in community capacity building (CLDMS, 2013). This has resulted in more activity by CLD practitioners focusing on individual outcomes: for example, improved literacy and numeracy; or positive destinations for young people. Although the CLD approach to adult learning and youth work is predicated on asset-based approaches, the focus for recent work has largely been directed by an agenda concerned with employability and curriculum for excellence.

Combined, this is problematic, as the aspiration for asset-based approaches is to work towards keeping people out of services for as long as possible, and striking the balance between traditional support delivered by agencies and that found naturally within networks and communities. If the benefits of asset-based approaches are to be realised, it is crucial to free up and empower staff to work actively towards supporting people so they consider how they can keep themselves well, rather than simply waiting until things reach crisis.

An example of a new model of delivery that supports practitioners to work autonomously with reduced paperwork and bureaucracy is shown in Figure 6.1, highlighting that asset-based approaches can happen and flourish within and across the context in which they are developed.

Figure 6.1: Case study – The Buurtzorg approach.

The Buurtzorg approach (meaning 'neighbourhood care') is a model of support that reports improved outcomes and high levels of satisfaction from both practitioners and those who are supported. The approach originated from one practitioner becoming increasingly frustrated with home care service delivery, so he eventually branched out to set up his own organisation. Buurtzorg was founded on the principle of being 'care-driven, instead of problem-driven', with the premise of giving nurses far greater control and autonomy over patient care.

There are six key services that make up the Buurtzorg model:
- holistic assessment;
- mapping the networks of informal care available;
- involvement of identified carers in the creation of the plan;
- delivery of care;
- providing support to the person in their own environment;
- promotion of the person's independence and self-care.

The model is underpinned by a nurse-led approach in which nurses work in small, self-managed and self-organised interdisciplinary teams (these comprise nurses and other allied health professionals). The nurses see fewer people and act as navigators to support people to find their own solutions to their care needs by drawing on the support of their networks. Crucially the nurses are supported by a back office who undertakes the necessary paperwork ensuring that bureaucracy is reduced and contact time between person and nurse is maintained.

The outcomes of this model are:

○ higher levels of patient satisfaction;
○ significant reductions in the cost of care provision;
○ development of a self-management structure for nurses.

Source: adapted from Ham and Brown, 2015; RCN, 2014

Mistrust

As has been acknowledged in previous chapters, it is problematic that asset-based approaches have received traction at the same time as efficiency savings and financial difficulties are endured. This has led many to be sceptical over whether or not the adoption of the approach is simply a device for making cuts to services, and shifting the responsibility for health and social welfare from the state to citizens (Ferguson, 2012; Friedli, 2012b). The danger is that the approach is seen as simply pushing responsibilities on to people and communities that may not have the skills and capacities to respond, a critique of the approach that was frequently highlighted by our interviewees:

> 'The financial imperative cancels out any real commitment to genuinely working with people … you're asking people to participate in a process of … the disinvestment of services. Then shifting responsibility of social welfare from the state to communities and individuals.' [academic]

Potential to exacerbate inequalities

In Scotland, although recent legislation for community empowerment has been passed (see in Chapter 1 for more detail) some commentators argue that a key issue is the extent to which the provisions of the legislation may serve to further empower those communities that are organised and influential, while not achieving meaningful change for marginalised or excluded ones or those with weak infrastructure (SCDC, 2014). These more marginalised communities may be unaware of the rights they will now have, or be aware of them but may not have the capacity to utilise them without support and advice. It could therefore be argued that there is an imperative for the state to take an active role in supporting community capacity building and helping to develop a strong community infrastructure (as described in Chapters 2 and 5) in disadvantaged neighbourhoods. If this type of support is not forthcoming, communities and individuals instructed to rely on their own assets may feel neglected and disenfranchised (Unwin, 2014).

Without the required and targeted support, asset-based initiatives at individual and community level pose the potential to exacerbate existing inequalities (Friedli, 2012b). The discussion at policy level on asset-based approaches, which reflects parallel discussions on 'social capital' (Collins and Feeney, 2014), often takes place in the context of disadvantaged people and communities. Rarely is it the case that interventions using asset-based approaches are designed with affluent communities in mind. As discussed in Chapter 1, legislation designed to empower communities may reinforce inequalities with well-organised, well-resourced ones most able to take advantage of new opportunities as they arise.

Given this context and new legislation, instead of seeing a move towards more investment in asset-based approaches, asset-based grass roots activity undertaken by community development practitioners continues to be under threat, and existing community-led organisations struggle to attract the income they need to respond independently to community needs (Collins and Feeney, 2014). Research investigating spending cuts trends across England and Scotland since 2010 highlights that the emerging pattern is for local authorities to direct shrinking resources towards protecting 'poor and vulnerable social groups from the most severe effects of austerity' (Hastings *et al.*, 2013, p. 4). Although laudable, these actions could have the consequence of taking resources away from preventative, health-promoting and community-led projects and could undermine the capacity of local authorities to provide a wide range of services 'across the social spectrum', leading to the withdrawal of services and supports with 'far-reaching implications for the nature and role of local government over the medium to longer term' (Hastings *et al.*, 2103, p. 35).

It can therefore be said that advocates of asset-based approaches are cautiously walking the tightrope between welcoming the act of rethinking the role of the state and taking the fall for 'an ideologically-driven shrinking of the state, with nothing left to replace it' (Crowther, 2014, p. 24).

Power

> 'Meaningful participation is simply not possible while there is no political will to alter current systems of power, responsibility and money' (Duffy, 2007, p. 35).

Commitment to asset-based approaches requires a real willingness on behalf of those who have power to share it. Truly embedding an asset-based approach therefore needs a change in the mindset of professionals, and people supported by services and communities, because it is about empowering everyone to be active and equal partners and requires capacity building both ways. This means every person in the system 'challenging and reconsidering their perceptions of themselves, their roles and of each other' (Durose *et al.*, 2013, p. 6).

If empowerment is a core value of policy it needs to be used to rebalance and not reinforce existing power relationships that may contribute to disadvantage. Policy and legislation will succeed in empowering communities only if it can prevent already powerful interests furthering their advantage at the expense of marginalised and excluded groups. Deprived or marginal communities remain so partly because they lack the power to make the case for the changes that they seek (SCDC, 2014). For such communities, empowerment is understood as a long-term, purposeful process that builds cohesion and confidence and establishes a social and organisational infrastructure (SCDC, 2014).

Governance structures and the distribution of power over who makes decisions are central to the ability to implement asset-based approaches at a community level. In Scotland there are thirty-two local authority areas and the average council serves around 178,000 people. By comparison Norway currently has 428 *kommuner* (councils) the average size of which is just 12,000 people. Turnout at Norwegian local elections is 64% – almost twice that of Scotland. One in eighty-one Norwegians stands in council elections compared to one in 2,071 Scots (Bryden and Refsgaard, 2015). The constraints in engaging local people in decision-making systems in local authorities of the scale we have in Scotland are obvious. Despite the move to a community-planning model and the development of various policy and legislative drivers designed to support increased participation in local decision-making processes (see Chapter 1), engagement by communities in decisions that affect them is not consistent or systematic. Furthermore there is little evidence to suggest community influence over how money is spent or how services are planned and delivered at local level despite these local structures and national imperatives (Garven *et al.*, 2014).

At a practitioner level, professional reluctance to give away status and control has been highlighted as one of the key challenges to asset-based principles, as is working becoming embedded in practice (Voorberg *et al.*, 2014). There could be a number of reasons for this, including the need to be accountable for targets and the fear of risk and change, as explored earlier. Building trust is particularly difficult in a situation where there is a power imbalance. For example, in a social work context, given the need to traverse the tensions between empowerment and safeguarding, practitioners may not be confident about sharing responsibility for risk if their organisation does not have a positive risk enablement culture and policies (SCIE, 2010). However Hopkins and Rippon (2015) suggest that lack of progress in implementing asset-based approaches has more to do with professional authority and the need to be seen as 'expert'. These researchers suggest that in some instances staff 'are unable to engage with the principles', and think that they 'know what is best' for the person they are supporting. This was commonly noted in our interviews:

> 'I think the common theme is it is still hard for professionals to overcome a need to be right, and I think in a way the more that is challenged, the more difficult the job becomes.' [NGO manager]

It should be recognised that there are many who have a vested interest in maintaining the status quo because it helps them maintain and retain their power base – however that manifests itself. Indeed there is evidence to indicate that those in governments or politics are often reluctant to give away too much power and control, and that in some instances there is a lack of trust from the public sector that those in the voluntary, third or private sector or communities themselves can actually deliver what is required (Richardson, 2011). On the other hand there is also said to be a growing sense of 'public disillusionment' with the public sector (Beresford, 2002), with citizens feeling mistrustful of official attempts to engage and involve them because of their history of lack of meaningful engagement and poor consultative experiences. This failure of trust in both directions is a key challenge in sustaining the collaborative relationships that are at the heart of the asset-based approaches.

Austerity

As highlighted earlier, the move towards asset-based approaches is based on the recognition that we need to work differently for improved outcomes and that we also know that efficiencies must be made. The potential is for policymakers, funders and providers to seize the chance to look 'up and out' to find new solutions and ways of doing things, become more willing to take and share risk with citizens and reconceptualise the meaning of 'resources' to value other types of contributions other than financial and monetary resources. This stance has the potential to enable public services to adopt different, collaborative ways of working such as asset-based approaches.

On the other hand, instead of seeing financial constraints as an opportunity to innovate, for some the reverse is true. There is emerging evidence that local authorities are responding by looking 'down and in', retrenching to protect statutory (not discretionary) services in order to meet their legal obligations (Asenova *et al.*, 2013) and focusing on those who are the most vulnerable (Hastings *et al.*, 2013). Some consider this a dangerous position as local authorities take more 'reactive cost saving measures that reduce rather than enhance their capacity to engage with local people and communities' (Miller and Whitehead, 2015, p. 1).

Barker (2010) states that there are two types of logic about how to make efficiencies to consider here. One is a 'substitutive logic', which asserts that 'the costs of providing public services can be moderated by shifting responsibilities from one provider … to another'. The other is 'additive' logic, which stresses that the 'long-term efficiencies in local public services will be delivered through bringing together existing resources and assets' (cited in Durose *et al.*, 2013, p. 14). Additive logic is more aligned with asset-based approaches in which people work increasingly in partnership to build on the strengths of each party. This thinking acknowledges that asset-based working is not an alternative to properly funded public services, but simply that it challenges how those services are designed and delivered (Hopkins and Rippon, 2015). Indeed Hambleton and Howard (2012, p. 17) caution against a primary focus on cost savings, stating:

> a 'more with less' approach to the current cutbacks in public spending is unlikely to be successful. Reaching out to other partners to create a grounded 'more with more' approach holds out greater promise.

Thus the focus becomes creating cross-sector collaborations to support locally embedded services and support (Munro, 2015).

There is evidence of both of these positions in the current climate; sometimes they are present simultaneously, with different parts of the same authority at various stages of the same process at the same time (Richardson, 2011; Asenova *et al.*, 2013; Hastings *et al.*, 2013). The reality is that strong disincentives to collaboration continue to exist (Kippen and Swinson Reid, 2014). The lack of available funding could be said to reinforce a competitive spirit, which results in organisations defending their own patch. For example, recent research highlights that, through competition (and competitive tendering more specifically), larger charities can threaten the existence of smaller grass-roots ones by 'knocking out' the smaller group (Locality, 2015).

Commissioning and contracting arrangements exert major influences and constraints for the delivery of asset-based approaches. Traditional patterns of procurement and tendering remain a significant issue, resulting in a narrower scope for agencies to do things differently (Foot and Hopkins, 2010). Slay and Penny (2014) describe the challenges in this dominant commissioning model as:

- ❍ taking a silo view, failing to take cognisance of the 'whole picture';

○ using only deficit-focused data, which targets only problems and avoids preventative spend options;

○ encouraging risk aversion by focusing on consistency rather than creativity;

○ fostering competition rather than collaboration;

○ being stifled by short-term gains – making short-term cost-efficiencies, which reduce the capacity for providers to develop approaches that could lead to longer-term change.

In reconsidering commissioning practices for asset-based approaches, the question for practitioners, funders and policy-makers has to be how to move away from one of 'producing' change towards how to 'facilitate' and 'stimulate' change together. The paradox here is that 'life' and 'empowered communities' cannot be bought, and nor can they be determined by those who sit on the periphery. Some say the best that commissioners can do, as detailed in the previous chapter, is to 'help create the conditions ... In that regard, sometimes the best thing an outside agency can do is get out of the way' (Russell, 2004).

In an attempt to shift power and influence over some elements of local spending, the Scottish government has recently invested support in training for community planning partners on participatory budgeting, often shortened to 'PB'. PB is a different way to allocate and manage public money, and to engage people in government, through a democratic process in which community members directly decide how to spend part of a public budget. It enables taxpayers to work with government to make the budget decisions that affect their lives. Originating in 1989 in Porto Alegre in Brazil, PB is now recognised internationally as a method through which citizens and communities can become involved in local decision-making processes in a meaningful and tangible way. In February 2015 Paris announced the biggest PB exercise in Europe, investing 20 million euros of their city budget and inviting citizens to submit proposals for spending priorities (Bruno, 2015). In Scotland the experience to date has been largely limited to small grants, some of which nonetheless have been able to produce positive outcomes (GCPH, 2012).

Scale and context

Achieving the shift towards asset-based approaches requires investment, and often it takes many years for savings and improved outcomes to be realised. In their discussion of co-production, Bovaird and Löeffler (2012) argue that: '[co-production] is value for money, but we cannot produce value without money' (cited in Pestoff *et al.*, 2012, p. 58).

Due to the need for an initial investment upfront, there is evidence that more preventative and community-based supports are often developed as 'pilots' or 'experiments' rather than as mainstream provision, and as such these often become destined to run alongside the interventions they are supposed to replace (ADASS, 2011). This raises critical questions regarding how these projects can be transitioned from the margins into the mainstream, a common issue highlighted in our interviews:

> 'People have too high expectations that projects and programmes will change things at a system level. We need to concentrate our energy on how we change the system itself.'
> [academic and advocacy practitioner]

If the focus is solely on the evidence from large-scale programmes, or pilot or test sites, there is a risk that the mainstream will regard the lessons learned as unrealistic (Kennedy *et al.*, 2014) or the product of special circumstances that are not seen as relevant or readily applicable. There may also be resistance to taking on board the approach because of: the lack of a dedicated budget or capacity for implementation; departmental silos which discourage sharing of resources; lack of appetite for change and risk (Nesta, 2012); or differences in the context and underpinning ideology of the approach. For example, in the field of community development, there has been some criticism of the way the asset-based community development (ABCD) (Kretzman and McKnight, 1993) approach, which originated in America, is currently being adopted in Scotland, with some academics questioning whether or not the starting point and operating context for ABCD and other asset-based approaches is the same. MacLeod and Emejulu (2014) postulate that the ABCD approach has at its heart values of individualisation, privatisation and a fundamental mistrust of the state. This contrasts directly to the Scottish context that we discussed in Chapter 1, where there is an increased focus on welfare, liberalism and collectivism and where there is a perception of state importance in protecting those who are the most vulnerable or marginalised in society. MacLeod and Emejulu (2014) suggest that the risk in adopting ABCD without an understanding of the underpinning ideology is that it may result in public issues (such as inequality and poverty) becoming privatised and a means to justify cuts to supports and services. These authors therefore caution against transplanting approaches from one place to another without a wider understanding of context. This was illustrated by one of our interviewees from an academic viewpoint:

> 'ABCD is very clear about being in opposition to the state. It sees the state as antagonistic, reproducing issues of weakness, brokenness and disease in people. We have the opposite in Scotland, where there is a much greater focus on understanding the role of the state in supporting people and groups who are so often excluded from society.' [academic]

For many, the notion of moving individual, localised approaches into the mainstream as part of a programme approach feels very much like a top-down imposition rather than a supported, bottom-up process, which enables responses to emerge organically from groups of people living and working within an area (Glasby *et al.*, 2013; Kennedy *et al.*, 2014). Indeed, a recent review of the evidence for scaling-up innovations found there to be heated debate about fidelity to specific models versus promoting emergence and adaption of models in different settings; both were viewed to be critical (Shiell-Davis, 2015). Asset-based approaches can be so heavily rooted in local context that many believe the outcomes or processes cannot therefore be applied in other areas. However there are many lessons that can be learnt and adapted such as how to successfully engage with different groups of people and understanding how and which participative approaches are useful in helping people think differently. For example, there has been an attempt to share the learning and values-based ways of working from large intensive interventions in healthcare and education services for specific target groups in Glasgow. Work is underway to extend the values and principles of this way of working to all staff and practitioners across whole services in an attempt to extend the reach and benefits of working in a more asset and strengths-based way (McLean *et al.*, in preparation).

More recently the thinking on asset-based approaches and co-production advocates less for 'scaling up' and more for 'scaling out, spreading ideas and innovation between organisations, enabling local innovation to flourish' (Durose *et al.*, 2013, p. 30), thereby ensuring the underpinning ethos is understood and the conditions are present that facilitate asset-based approaches to become practically embedded. Indeed Hopkins and Rippon (2015) suggest that it is too early a stage for asset-based approaches to be mainstreamed:

> Changing to an asset-based approach offers and creates a new relational perspective. It is not a set of tools or techniques that can be applied without a change in organisational culture and individual practice. It must be a process, not a top-down plan (Hopkins and Rippon, 2015, p. 23).

If the belief in working 'with' – not 'on' or 'for' – people and communities is embedded within practice, then it follows that thinking about scale should be done in partnership with those who are involved and who will be impacted by the change. As such, the emphasis becomes a move away from attempting to identify fixed answers and increasing the number of people adopting the solution, and one towards creating spaces where responses can be explored, designed and owned locally as issues arise. Conceptualising asset-based approaches in this manner places greater emphasis on practitioners and people continually enquiring together to validate how they relate to each other and work together. This is likely to require new forms of facilitation within and across organisational boundaries (GCPH and SCDC, 2015b). It also has the benefit of being able to develop context-appropriate practice and 'reflects citizen preferences for "small scale, informal activities" ' (Durose *et al.*, 2013).

Conclusion

There is growing consensus that asset-based approaches are a vital part of a progressive approach to improving outcomes for people and communities, but undertaking this work is complex, time- and resource-intensive and countercultural to how many public service organisations currently operate. Throughout this chapter we have demonstrated some of the ways in which asset-based approaches fundamentally challenge the established structural, behavioural and cultural ways of practice that are key features of our existing model of public health and social service delivery.

To overcome these difficulties and to enable people to practise 'the change they seek', space and time within their roles must be provided to allow for learning and reflection, and organisations and cultures must integrate their knowledge and expertise with successful examples of good practice alongside the experience and knowledge of those who they support or work with in communities.

REFLECTION

Throughout this book we have sought to examine the nature of asset-based approaches and the evidence base for their impact in achieving improved outcomes for people and communities. We have discussed what supports asset-based approaches so they are effective and what constrains them, and we have provided some examples of asset-based working in practice.

As discussed in our introduction, the increased attention to asset-based working has largely come about through the recognition that the current models of delivery of public services are no longer effective in addressing the causes of ill health and poor quality of life outcomes in the twenty-first century; nor are they, in many instances, sustainable or desirable.

We chose to concentrate our discussion mainly within a Scottish context, but where possible have drawn learning from the UK and beyond. The current political and policy landscape in Scotland is conducive to asset-based approaches with its renewed emphasis on 'shifting the balance of power'. Alongside prevention, citizen involvement and democratic participation are at the core of the public service reform agenda. Across the major policy areas of health, social services, regeneration and social justice, ideas and proposals are emerging which support ways of working with people which support them to be 'part of the solution' rather than problems to be fixed.

A balanced view

That said, the wider social and political context of poverty and inequality, in Scotland and on a global level, means that asset-based approaches will not address the root causes of structural health and social inequalities, nor will they, on their own, mitigate the worst impacts of entrenched poverty and social division. We need always to remind ourselves of what is realistic for asset-based approaches to be able to deliver.

either are asset-based approaches a universal panacea, nor ropriate to adopt uncritically and in all circumstances. It is ident that some public services are more suitable for asset-based working than others. At one end of the service delivery spectrum – in intensive care or accident and emergency settings, for example – asset-based working is less of a priority than technical excellence, effectiveness and efficiency of care. In many other domains however there remains the potential for health and social services to be effective in empowering individuals and communities to take control over their circumstances and for health and social services to reorientate and reshape care delivery to support people to be co-producers of health and well-being rather than simply consumers of services.

Throughout the text we have touched on the difficulties of the language of asset-based approaches, and we recognise that some may consider asset-based approaches a slightly vague concept given the wide variety of different approaches and processes encapsulated in the term. Much confusion still exists over what is meant by the term 'asset-based approaches' and whether it means the same or is different to established models of participatory practice. For good or bad, theories and language change with the fashions of the day, but, if we believe in the central tenets of self-determination and individual and collective empowerment, it is vital to ensure that the underlying values, principles and the focus on relationships, which underpin this approach, are not lost the next time the language moves on.

Despite difficulties with the language and in some cases concerns about the imperatives for moving towards an asset-based approach to public services, there is growing momentum in Scotland for this way of working. This has been influenced at least in part by the endorsing policy environment that has given this work increasingly high priority, and also critically by practitioner willingness to engage in the approach. It could be said that practitioners intuitively gravitate to an asset-based way of working because it builds on the tradition of relationship-based practice and reflects the underpinning core values of community development, public health and social services professions. Arguably the focus on values could be considered the most important impetus for this way of working.

The values and principles associated with asset-based approaches honour and elevate the perceptions and experiences of people – those who have the sharpest focus on what matters most in their lives and in their communities. A move towards asset-based working reflects a commitment to operate in a different way: to involve people, to take risks, to transfer power and to facilitate and enable rather than provide. For asset-based approaches to be effective, we need to examine inhibitive cultures, systems and processes that still exist within many public service organisation and find ways to adopt a different culture, which allows transfer of power and which embraces new measures of success. We need to find ways to free up our workforce to enable them to share control alongside those they support, and we must enhance and develop skill sets appropriate to this way of working.

In the course of researching this book, we have found evidence of progress towards asset-based approaches. There are pockets of activity across Scotland and around the world that reflect the emerging understanding of what it takes to enable asset-based approaches to flourish, as described in Chapter 5. Although developments continue to emerge, the evidence signals that there is no one easy answer to overcoming the broader challenges at structural and systems level if the approach is to reach its proposed transformational potential. It is unsurprising, given the emerging nature and associated challenges of both researching and measuring asset-based approaches, that this review shows little evidence of the medium- to longer-term outcomes of the approach. A focus on strengthening the research base as well as the status of the evidence is vital.

In Scotland the energy for asset-based approaches has been ideologically driven by the acknowledgement of the need for different ways of working and aspirations for a 'good and equal society', which is fundamentally driven by values rather than evidence. In a time of financial constraint, we need to be able to reconceptualise our vision for success and prosperity as a society, and to consider who holds the power for transformative change. We should think about how to make better use of the resources we already have, and we need to redirect energy and money away from what we know does not work. There is an opportunity to build on the momentum described earlier, to establish collaborations across agencies and communities and begin to create the conditions described in Chapter 5 in order to affect the narrative and to move this thinking from rhetoric to action. Real change has to be accompanied by investment and commitment to moving resources to people who use services, to communities and to frontline staff.

Looking to the future

To adopt an asset-based approach is to build on strengths and hope. At a UK level, some civil society leaders are instigating a 'call to action for the common good' (Crowther, 2014), with the aim of 'building an inspiring and convincing national story of hope' (Call to Action for the Common Good, n.d.) and challenging the current consensus. This appeal is based on our belief that we can solve society's big problems only if we unlock the potential of people and institutions working together for the common good. In a Scottish context there is much to be hopeful for – national conversations are taking place on how to achieve a fairer, healthier and more socially just Scotland, while Scottish citizens are calling for more democratic participation, and more legislation supporting individual and community empowerment is in the pipeline. But change at a structural and systems level takes time, energy, an appetite for risk and a commitment to be a learning society – are we ready for the long game?

REFERENCES

Adams, A. and Bond, S. (2000) 'Hospital nurses' job satisfaction, individual and organisational characteristics', *Journal of Advanced Nursing*, Vol. 32, No. 3, pp. 536–43

ADASS Eastern region (2011) *Investing in Prevention for Older People at the Health and Social Care Interface*, Oxford: Oxford Brookes University, Institute of Public Care. Available from URL: https://ipc.brookes.ac.uk/ publications/pdf/Investing_in_prevention_for_older_people_at_the_ health_and_social_care_interface.pdf (accessed 15 February 2016)

Aked, J., Marks, N., Cordon, C. and Thompson, S. (2008) *Five Ways to Wellbeing: The Evidence*, London: New Economics Foundation

Alford, J. (2009) *Engaging Public Sector Clients: From Service Delivery to Co-Production*, Basingstoke: Palgrave

Allcock, A., Dormon, F., Taunt, R. and Dixon J. (2015) *Constructive Comfort: Accelerating Change in the NHS*, London: The Health Foundation

Allen, K. and Glasby, J. (2010) *The Billion Dollar Question: Embedding Prevention in Older People's Services – 10 'High Impact' Changes*, HSMC policy paper 8, Birmingham: HSMC

Alliance Scotland (2013) *Being Human: A Human Rights Based Approach to Health and Social Care in Scotland*, Glasgow: Alliance Scotland

Alvarez-Dardet, C., Morgan, A., Ruiz Cantero, M. T. and Hernan, M. (2015) 'Improving the evidence base on public health assets – the way ahead: A proposed research agenda', *Journal of Epidemiology Community Health*, Vol. 69, No. 8, pp. 721–3

Andrews, N., Driffield, D. and Poole, V. (2009) 'A collaborative and relationship-centred approach to improving assessment and care management with older people in Swansea', *Quality in Ageing*, Vol. 10, No. 3, pp. 12–23

Antonovsky, A. (1987) *Unraveling The Mystery of Health – How People Manage Stress and Stay Well*, San Francisco: Jossey-Bass

Antonovsky, A. (1993) 'The structure and properties of the sense of coherence scale', *Social Science and Medicine*, Vol. 36, pp. 725–33

Antonovsky, A. and Sagy, S. (1986) 'The development of a sense of coherence and its impact on responses to stress situations', *Journal of Social Psychology*, Vol. 126, pp. 213–25

Arnaboldi, M., Lapsley, I. and Steccolini, P. (2015) 'Performance management in the public sector: The ultimate challenge', *Financial Accountability and Management*, Vol. 31, No. 1, pp. 1–22

Asenova, D., Bailey, S. J. and McCann, C. (2013) *Managing the Social Risks of Public Spending Cuts in Scotland*, York: Joseph Rowntree Foundation

Asquith, S., Clark, C. and Waterhouse, L. (2005) *The Role of the Social Worker in the twenty-first century*, Edinburgh: Scottish Executive

Audit Scotland (2014) *Reshaping Care for Older People*, Edinburgh: Audit Scotland

Baker, D. (2014) 'Developing and implementing a robust asset-based approach to public health', *Perspectives in Public Health*, Vol. 134, p. 129

Barker, A. (2010) *Co-Production of Local Public Services*, London: Local Authorities Research Council Initiative

Barr, A. (2014) *Community Development – Everyone's Business?*, Glasgow: Scottish Community Development Centre

Barr, A. and Hashagen, A. (2000) *ABCD Handbook: A Framework for Evaluating Community Development*, London: Community Development Foundation

Barr, A., Drysdale, J., Purcell, R. and Ross, C. (1995) *Strong Communities Effective Government, the Role of Community Work*, Glasgow: Scottish Community Development Centre

Barrie, K. and Miller, E. (2015) 'Measuring personal outcomes in service settings: Collected briefings from the meaningful and measurable' (online). Available from URL: https://meaningfulandmeasurable.wordpress.com/project-outputs (accessed 30 September 2015)

Beeston, C., McCartney, G., Ford, J., Wimbush, E., Beck, S., MacDonald, W. and Fraser, A. (2013) *Health Inequalities Policy Review for the Scottish Ministerial Task Force on Health Inequalities*, Glasgow: NHS Health Scotland

Beresford, P. (2002) 'Participation and social policy: Transformation, liberation or regulation?', in Sykes, R., Bochel, C. and Ellison, N. (eds) (2002) *Social Policy Review 14: Developments and Debates 2001–2002*, Bristol: Policy Press

Bovaird, T. and Löeffler, E. (2012) 'The role of co-production in health and social care: why we need to change', in Löeffler, E., Power, G., Bovaird, T. and Hine-Hughes, F. (eds) (2012) *Co-Production in Health and Social Care. What It Is and How To Do It*, Birmingham: Governance International and Joint Health Improvement Team, Scottish Government

Boyle, D., Slay, J. and Stephens, L. (2010) *Public Services Inside Out: Putting Co-Production Into Practice*, London: Nesta

Brotchie, J. (2013) *The Enabling State: From Rhetoric to Reality. Case Studies of Contemporary Practice*, Dunfermline: The Carnegie Trust

Brun, C. and Rapp, R. C. (2001) 'Strengths-based case management: Individuals' perspectives on strengths and the case manager relationship', *Social Work*, Vol. 46, No. 3, pp. 278–88

Bruno, E. (2015) *Co-Deciding with Citizens: Towards Digital Democracy at EU Level*, Brussels: European Citizen Action Service

Bunt, L. and Harris, M. (2009) *The Human Factor: How Transforming Health Care to Involve the Public Can Save Money and Save Lives*, London: Nesta

Burns, H. (2013) 'Assets for health', in Löeffler, E., Power, G., Bovaird, T. and Hine-Hughes, F. (eds) (2013) *Co-Production of Health and Wellbeing in Scotland*, Birmingham: Governance International

Bryden, J. and Refsgaard, K. (2015) *Local Government in the Nordic Countries, and Contemporary Reform Proposals in Norway*, Edinburgh: Nordic Horizons

Cairney, P. (2015) 'Evidence based best practice is more political than it looks: a case study of the "Scottish approach"' (online). Available from URL: https://paulcairney.files.wordpress.com/2015/06/cairney-2015-ebpm-and-best-practice-22–4-15.pdf (accessed 4 February 2016)

Call to Action for the Common Good (n.d.) 'Welcome to a story of hope' (online). Available from URL: www.calltoactionforthecommongood.org.uk/post/118769034504/welcome-to-a-story-of-hope (accessed 9 January 2016)

Calouste Gulbenkian Foundation (1968) *Community Work and Social Change. A Report on Training*, London: Longman

Campbell, J. and Oliver, M. (1996) *Disability Politics: Understanding Our Past, Changing Our Future*, London: Routledge

Carpenter, J., Webb, C., Bostock, L. and Coomber, C. (2012) *SCIE Research Briefing 43: Effective supervision in social work and social care*, London: Social Care Institute for Excellence

CeVe Scotland (1990) *Training for Change: A Report on Community Education Training*, Edinburgh: Scottish Community Education Council

Chapin, R., Nelson-Becker, H. and Macmillan, K. (2006) 'Strengths-based and solutions-focused approaches to practice', in Berkman, B. and D'Ambruoso, S. (eds) (2006) *Handbook of Social Work in Health and Aging*, Oxford: Oxford University Press

Chapin, R. K., Nelson-Becker, H., Macmillan, K. and Sellon, A. (2015) 'Strengths based and solution focused approaches to practice with older adults', in (2015) Kaplan, D. B. and Berkman, B., *The Oxford Handbook of Social Work in Health and Aging* (2nd edn), Oxford: Oxford University Press

Christiansen, J. and Bunt, L. (2012) *Innovation in Policy: Allowing for Creativity, Social Complexity and Uncertainty in Public Governance*, London: Nesta

Christie, C. (2011) *Commission on the Future Delivery of Public Services*, Edinburgh: APS Group Scotland

CLDMS (2013) *Community Learning and Development in Scottish Local Authorities*, Glasgow: Community Learning and Development Managers Scotland

Cobban, N. (2004) 'Improving domiciliary care for people with dementia and their carers: The raising the standard project', in Innes, A., Archibald, C. and Murphy, C. (eds) (2004) *Dementia and Social Inclusion*, London: Jessica Kingsley

Coffey, M. and Coleman, M. (2001) 'The relationship between support and stress in forensic community mental health nursing', *Journal of Advanced Nursing*, Vol. 34, No. 3, pp. 397–407

Collins, C. and Feeney, M. (2014) *Tea in the Pot – Building Social Capital or a 'Great Good Place' in Govan?*, Paisley: University of the West of Scotland

Cook, A. and Miller, E. (2012) *Talking Points: Personal Outcomes Approach, Practical Guide*, Edinburgh: Joint improvement Tea

Coote, A., Allen, J. and Woodhead, D. (2004) *Finding Out What Works: Building Knowledge about Complex, Community-Based Initiatives,* London: Kings Fund

CoSLA (2014) *Commission on Strengthening Local Democracy Final Report,* Edinburgh: CoSLA

Craig, P., Dieppe, P., Macintyre, S., Mitchie, S., Nazareth, I., Petticrew, M. (2008) 'Developing and evaluating complex interventions: The new Medical Research Council guidance', *BMJ,* Vol. 337, pp. 979–83

Crowther, N. (2014) *A Call to Action for the Common Good,* Dunfermline: Carnegie UK Trust

Curtice, M. J. and Exworthy, T. (2010) 'FREDA: A human rights-based approach to healthcare', *The Psychiatrist,* Vol. 34, pp. 150–6

Dailly, J. and Barr, A. (2008) *Meeting the Shared Challenge: Understanding a Community-Led Approach to Health Improvement,* Glasgow: Scottish Community Development Centre

Department of Health (2012) *Caring for Our Future: Reforming Care and Support,* London: Department of Health

Department of Health (2014) *Wellbeing and Why It Matters to Health Policy,* London: Department of Health

Dewar, B. and Sharp, C. (2013) 'Appreciative dialogue for co-facilitation in action research and practice development', *International Practice Development Journal,* Vol. 3, No. 2, p. 7

Diener, E. and Seligman, M. E. (2002) 'Very happy people', *Psychological Science,* Vol. 13, No. 1, pp. 81–4

Drumm, M. (2012) *Culture Change in the Public Sector,* IRISS Insights No 17, Glasgow: Institute for Research and Innovation in Social Services. Available from URL: www.iriss.org.uk/sites/default/files/iriss-insight-17.pdf (accessed 31 July 2015)

Drumm, M. (2013) *The Role of Personal Storytelling in Practice,* IRISS Insights 23, Glasgow: Institute for Research and Innovation in Social Services

Duffy, S. (2007) 'Participative public services', in Parker, S. and Parker, S. (eds) (2007) *Unlocking Innovation: Why Citizens Hold the Key to Public Sector Reform,* London: Demos

Duffy, S. and Fulton, K. (2010) *Architecture for Personalisation,* Sheffield: The Centre for Welfare Reform

Duncan, B. L. and Miller, S. D. (2000) *The Heroic Client: Doing Client-Directed Outcome-Informed Therapy,* San Francisco: Jossey-Bass

Durose, C., Mangan, C., Needham, C. and Rees, J. (2013) *Transforming Local Public Services Through Co-Production,* Birmingham: University of Birmingham

Durose, C., Mangan, C., Needham, C. and Rees, J. (2014) *Evaluating Co-Production: Pragmatic Approaches to Building the Evidence Base,* Birmingham: University of Birmingham

Early, T. J. and Glenmaye, L. F. (2000) 'Valuing families: Social work practice with families from a strengths perspective', *Social Work,* Vol. 45, pp. 118–30

Education Scotland (2015) *Working with Scotland's Communities – A Survey of Who Does Community Learning and Development,* Glasgow: Education Scotland

Egan, M., Tannahill, C., Bond, L., Kearns, A. and Mason, P. (2014) *The Links between Regeneration and Health: A GoWell Research Synthesis (March*

2013), Glasgow: GoWell

Elvidge, J. (2011) *Northern Exposure – Lessons from the First Twelve Years of Devolved Government in Scotland*, London: Institute for Government

Elvidge, J. (2014) *A Route Map to an Enabling State*, Dunfermline: Carnegie UK

Emejulu, A. (2015) *Community Development in Contradictory Times*, Glasgow: Scottish Community Development Centre

Equality Trust (2015) 'The scale of economic inequality in the UK' (online). Available from URL: https://www.equalitytrust.org.uk/scale-economic-inequality-uk (accessed 11 January 2016)

Eriksson, M. and Lindström, B. (2006) 'Antonovsky's sense of coherence scale and the relation with health: A systematic review', *Journal of Epidemiology and Community Health*, Vol. 60, No. 5, pp. 376–81

Escobar, O. (2014) 'Towards participatory democracy in Scotland' (online). Available from URL: http://postmag.org/towards-participatory-democracy-in-scotland (accessed 31 August 2015)

Ferguson, I. (2012) 'Personalisation, social justice and social work: A reply to Simon Duffy', *Journal of Social Work Practice: Psychotherapeutic Approaches in Health, Welfare and the Community*, Vol. 26, No. 1, pp. 55–73; doi: 10.1080/02650533.2011.623771

Findlay, E. (2015) *Analytical Paper on Co-Production*, Edinburgh: Scottish Government, Office of the Chief Social Policy Advisor

Fischbacher, C., McCartney, G., McAllister, D. and Lawson, K. (2013) *The Dog That Didn't Bark – Where Is the Public Debate on Assets Approaches*, abstract, paper presented at Scottish Faculty of Public Health Conference, Dunblane. Available from URL: www.fphscotconf.co.uk/uploads/fph2013-abstracts/FPH2013–1305.pdf (accessed 15 February 2016)

Foot, J. (2012) 'What makes us healthy? The asset approach in practice: evidence, action and evaluation' (online). Available from URL: www.asset-basedconsulting.co.uk/uploads/publications/wmuh.pdf (accessed 30 June 2015)

Foot, J. and Hopkins, T. (2010) *A Glass Half Full: How an Asset Approach Can Improve Community Health and Wellbeing*, London: Improvement and Development Agency

Francis, A. P. (2014) 'Strengths-based assessments and recovery in mental health: Reflections from practice', *International Journal of Social Work and Human Services Practice*, Vol. 2, No. 6, pp. 264–71

Friedli, L. (2012a) 'What we've tried, hasn't worked': The politics of asset-based public health', *Critical Public Health*, Vol. 23, No. 2, pp. 131–45

Friedli, L. (2012b) 'Always look on the bright side: The rise of asset-based approaches', *Scottish Anti-Poverty Review*, Winter 2011/12, pp. 11–15

Fry, D. (2009) *Measuring What Matters Conference Report*, Fife: International Association for Community Development

Gamsu, M. (2015) 'Asset based working – it's not just the community bit around the edges' (blog post online). Available from URL: http://localdemocracyandhealth.com/2015/04/27/asset-based-working-its-not-just-the-community-bit-around-the-edges (accessed 31 August 2015)

Garven, F., Grimes, A., Mitchell, J. and Whittam, G. (2014) 'Community engagement, procurement and community action: Research report for the National Community Planning Group', unpublished

GCPH (2011) *Asset-Based Approaches for Health Improvement: Redressing the Balance*, Briefing Paper 9 Concept Series, Glasgow: Glasgow Centre for Population Health

GCPH (2012) *Putting Asset-Based Approaches in Practice: Identification, Mobilisation and Measurement of Assets*, Briefing Paper Concept Series 10, Glasgow: Glasgow Centre for Population Health

GCPH (2014) *Towards Asset-Based Health and Care Services*, Briefing Paper 13 Concept Series, Glasgow: Glasgow Centre for Population Health

GCPH and SCDC (2015a) *Animating Assets. Insight Report: Progress and Learning So Far*, Glasgow: Glasgow Centre for Population Health and the Scottish Community Development Centre

GCPH and SCDC (2015b) *Positive Conversations, Meaningful Change: Learning from Animating Assets*, Final Report, Glasgow: Glasgow Centre for Population Health and the SCDC. Available from URL: www.gcph.co.uk/ work_themes/theme_4_assets_and_resilience/health_improvement_asset_ based_approaches/animating_assets (accessed 30 November 2015)

Glasby, J. (2011) 'From evidence-based to knowledge-based policy and practiced', in Glasby, J (ed.) (2011) *Evidence, Policy and Practice*, Bristol: Policy Press

Glasby, J. and Beresford, P. (2006) 'Who knows best? Evidence-based practice and the service user contribution', *Critical Social Poli*cy, Vol. 26, No. 1, pp. 268–84

Glasby, J., Miller, R. and Lynch, J. (2013) *Turning the Welfare State Upside Down? Developing a New Adult Social Care Offer*, HSMC Policy Paper 15, Birmingham: University of Birmingham, Health Services Management Centre. Available from URL: www.birmingham.ac.uk/Documents/ college-social-sciences/social-policy/HSMC/publications/PolicyPapers/ policy-paper-fifteen.pdf (accessed 15 February 2016)

Glasgow Disability Alliance (2012) 'About Glasgow Disability Alliance (GDA)' (online). Available from URL: www.gdaonline.co.uk/about/index. php (accessed 11 January 2016)

GoWell (2007) *The Regeneration Challenge in Transformation Areas. Evidence from the GoWell Baseline Survey 2006*, Glasgow: GoWell

GoWell (2014) *Context Briefing 1. Changes in Population, Deprivation and Health*, Glasgow: GoWell

Graeber, D. (2015) *The Utopia of Rules: On Technology, Stupidity, and the Secret Joys of Bureaucracy*, Brooklyn, NY: Melville House

Greenwood, D. J. (2015) 'An analysis of the theory/concept entries in the SAGE *Encyclopedia of Action Research*: What we can learn about action research in general form the encyclopedia', *Action Research*, Vol. 13, No. 2, pp. 198–213

Griffiths, S. and Foley, B. (2009) *Collective Co-Production: Working Together to Improve Public Services*, Swindon: Local Authorities and Research Councils Initiative

Griffiths, S., Foley, B. and Prendergast, J. (2009) *Assertive Citizens: New Relationships in the Public Services, [place of publication]*: Social Market Foundation supported by Price Waterhouse Coopers

Hallsworth, M. with Parker, S and Rutter, J. (2011) *Policy Making in the Real World: Evidence and Analysis*, London: Institute for Government

Ham, C. and Brown, A. (2015) *The Future is Here.* London: The Kings Fund

Hambleton, R. and Howard, J. (2012) *Place-Based Leadership and Public Service Innovation*, Bristol: Centre for Sustainable Planning and Environments, Department of Planning and Architecture, University of the West of England

Hanlon, P. and Carlisle, S. (n.d.) 'Modernity in crisis' (online). Available from URL: www.afternow.co.uk/sites/default/files/Modernity%20In%20 Crisis%20Summary%20Paper.pdf (accessed 30 June 2015)

Harrison, D., Ziglio, E., Levin, L. and Morgan, A. (2004) *Assets for Health and Development: Developing a Conceptual Framework*, Venice: World Health Organisation, European Office for Investment for Health and Development

Harvie, P. (2014) 'It's time for us Scot's to make up and rebuild our fragile society together', *Sunday Post*, 21 September

Hastings, A. and Matthews, P. (2011) *Sharp Elbows: Do the Middle-Classes Have Advantages in Public Service Provisions and If So How?*, Glasgow: University of Glasgow

Hastings, A., Bailey, N., Bramley, K., Gannon, G. and Watkins, D. (2013) *Coping with the Cuts? Local Government and Poorer Communities*, York: Joseph Rowntree Foundation

Health Foundation (2011) *Improvement Science*, London: The Health Foundation

Helmer, M., Pullar, V. and Carter, E. (2014) 'Social work and diversional therapy: Common threads from a strengths perspective', *International Journal of Social Work and Human Services Practice*, Vol. 2, No. 6, pp. 296–302

HELP (2012) 'Empowering communities for health' (online). Available from URL: www.healthempowerment.co.uk/wp-content/uploads/2012/11/DH_report_Nov_2011.pdf (accessed 30 September 2015)

Hills, M. and Mullett, J. (2000) 'Community-based research: Creating evidence-based practice for health and social change' (online). Available from URL: www.leeds.ac.uk/educol/documents/00001388.htm (accessed 31 August 2015)

HMSO (1975) *Adult Education: The Challenge of Change (The Alexander Report).* Edinburgh: HMSO

Hopkins, T. and Rippon, S. (2015) *Head, Hands and Heart: Asset-Based Approaches in Health Care – A Review of the Conceptual Evidence and Case Studies of Asset-Based Approaches in Health, Care and Wellbeing*, London: The Health Foundation

Hornstrup, C. and Johansen, T. (2009) 'From appreciative inquiry to inquiring appreciatively', *Appreciative Practitioner*, Vol. 11, No. 3, pp. 7–14

Housden, P. (2014) 'This is us', *Civil Service Quarterly*, Vol. 4. Available from URL: https://quarterly.blog.gov.uk/2014/04/16/this-is-us (accessed 31 July 2015)

House of Commons Library (2013) 'Standard note SN/SG/1467', July

Hunter, D., Marks, L. and Smith, K. (2010) *The Public Health System in England*, Bristol: The Policy Press

Ibrahim, N., Michail, M. and Callaghan, P. (2014) 'The strengths based approach as a service delivery model for severe mental illness: A meta-analysis of clinical trials' (online). Available from URL: http://link.springer.com/article/10.1186%2Fs12888–014–0243–6 (accessed 15 February 2016)

Inequality Briefing (2014) 'The richest 1% of the UK population have as much wealth as the poorest 55% combined' (online), Briefing 48. Available from URL: http://inequalitybriefing.org/brief/briefing-48-the-richest-1-of-the-uk-population-have-as-much-wealth-as-the-p (accessed 31 July 2015)

Inglis, J. (2013) *Social Assets in Action: Evaluation Report*, Glasgow: Institute for Research and Innovation in Social Services

Innes, A., Macpherson, S. and McCabe, L. (2006) *Promoting Person-Centred Care at the Frontline*, York: Joseph Rowntree Foundation

Jackson, T. (2011) *Prosperity Without Growth: Economies for a Finite Planet*, London: Earthscan

Jenkinson, C. E., Dickens, A. P., Jones, K., Thompson-Coon, J, Taylor, R.S., Rogers, M., Bambra, C. L., Lang, I. and Richards, S. H. (2013) 'Is volunteering a public health intervention? A systematic review and meta-analysis of the health and survival of volunteers', *BMC Public Health*, Vol. 13, No. 1, p. 773

Kemshall, H. (2002) *Risk, Social Policy and Welfare*, Buckingham: Open University Press

Kennedy, A., Rogers, A., Chew-Graham, C., Blakeman, T., Bowen, R. and Gardner, C. (2014) 'Implementation of a self-management support approach (WISE) across a health system: a process evaluation explaining what did and did not work for organisations, clinicians and patients', *Implementation Science*, Vol. 9, p. 129

Kippen, H. and Swinson Reid, R. (2014) *From Providers to Partners: What Will it Take?*, Edinburgh: Coalition of Care and Support Providers in Scotland

Kivimaki, M., Elovainio, M. and Vahtera, J. (2000) 'Workplace bullying and sickness absence in hospital staff', *Occupational and Environmental Medicine*, Vol. 57, No. 10, pp. 656–60

Kretzman, J. P. and McKnight, J. L. (1993) *Building Communities from the Inside Out: A Path Toward Finding and Mobilizing a Communities Assets*, Chicago, IL: Institute for Policy Research

Krishnadas, R., McLean, J., Batty, D. G., Burns, H., Deans, K. A., Ford, I., McConnachie, A., McLean, J. S., Millar, K., Sattar, N., Shiels, P. G., Velupillai, Y. N., Packard, C. J. and Cavanagh, J. (2013) 'Socio-economic deprivation and cortical morphology: Psychological, social and biological determinants of ill health study', *Psychosomatic Medicine*, Vol. 75, No. 7, pp. 616–23

Latchford, P. (2011) 'They moved like fish: The Birmingham riots' (online). Available from URL: www.yumpu.com/en/document/view/11653701/they-moved-like-fish (accessed 15 February 2016)

Leyland, A. H., Dundas, R., McLoone, P., Boddy, F. A. (2007) *Inequalities in Mortality in Scotland 1981–2001*, Glasgow: MRC Social and Public Health

Sciences Unit

Lietz, C. (2009) 'Establishing evidence for strengths-based interventions? Reflections from social work's research conference', *Social Work*, Vol. 54, No. 1, pp. 85–7

Lindström, B. and Eriksson, M. (2005) 'Salutogenesis', *Journal of Epidemiology and Community Health*, Vol. 59, No. 6, pp. 440–2

Lindström, B. and Eriksson, M. (2009) 'The salutogenic approach to the making of HiAP/healthy public policy: Illustrated by a case study', *Global Health Promotion*, Vol. 16, No. 1, pp. 17–28

Lindström, B. and Eriksson, M. (2010) *The Hitchhikers Guide to Salutogenesis. Salutogenic Pathways to Health Promotion*, Folkhälsan Health Promotion Research Report 2. Helsinki: Folkhälsan Research Centre, Health Promotion Research

Locality (2015) *Keep It Local for Better Services,* London: Locality

Loney, M. (1983) *Community Against Government: The British Community Development Project (1968–78)*, London: Heinemann

McCartney, G. (2011) 'Illustrating health inequalities in Glasgow', *Journal of Epidemiology and Community Health*, Vol. 65, No. 1, p. 94

MacGregor, A., McConville, S. and Maxwell, M. (2014) *WRAP Groups within a Feasibility Study: Qualitative Report*, Edinburgh: ScotCen Social Research

MacIntyre, S., MacIver, S. and Sooman A. (1993) 'Area, class and health: Should we be focusing on places or people?', *Journal of Social Policy*, Vol. 22, No. 2 (April), pp. 213–34; doi: 10.1017/S0047279400019310

McLaughlin, K. (2007) 'Regulation and risk in social work: The General Social Care Council and the Social Care Register in context', *British Journal of Social Work*, Vol. 37, No. 7, pp. 1263–77

McLean, J. and McNeice, V. (2012) *Assets in Action: Illustrating Asset-Based Approaches for Health Improvement*, Glasgow: Glasgow Centre for Population Health

McLean, J., Mitchell, C. and McNeice, V. (in preparation) 'Working title: Illustrating asset-based approaches in service settings', Glasgow; Glasgow Centre for Population Health

MacLeod, J. and Nelson, G. (2000) 'Programs for the promotion of family wellness and the prevention of child maltreatment: A meta-analytic review', *Child Abuse and Neglect*, Vol. 24, No. 9, pp. 1127–49

MacLeod, M. A. and Emejulu, A. (2014) 'Neoliberalism with a community face? A critical analysis of asset-based community development in Scotland', *Journal of Community Practice*, Vol. 22, No. 4, pp. 430–50

Maher, S. (2015) *Health Improvement Scotland: Co-Production and Improvement Methodology*, Glasgow: Institute for Research and Innovation in Social Services. Available from URL: http://irissfm.iriss.org.uk/episode/134 (accessed 30 September 2015)

Mair, C., Zdeb, K. and Markie, K. (2011) *Making Better Places Making Places Better: the Distribution of Positive and Negative Outcomes in Scotland*, Edinburgh: Improvement Service. Available from URL: www.improvementservice.org.uk/assets/making-better-places.pdf (accessed 31 July 2015)

Marmot, M. (2010) *Fair Society, Healthy Lives: Strategic Review of Health Inequalities in England post 2010*, London: Institute of Health Equity

Marsh, P. and Fisher, S. (2010) *Developing the Evidence Base for Social Work and Social Care Practice*, Bristol: The Policy Press

Mason, A., Tetley, J. and Urqhuart, G. (2006) 'Community care in Scotland', in Beech, J., Hand, O., Mulhern, M. and Weston, J. (eds) (2006) *Scottish Life and Society: The Individual and Community Life. A compendium of Scottish Ethnology*, Edinburgh: Birlinn

Mayne, J. (2001) 'Addressing attribution through contribution analysis: Using performance measures sensibly', *The Canadian Journal of Program Evaluation*, Vol. 16, No. 1, pp. 1–24

Mguni, N. and Bacon, N. (2010) *Taking the Temperature of Local Communities: The Wellbeing and Resilience Measure (WARM)*, The Young Foundation Local Wellbeing Project, London: The Young Foundation

Miller, E. (2010) 'Can the shift from needs-led to outcomes-focused assessment in health and care deliver on policy priorities?', *Research, Policy and Planning*, Vol. 28, No. 2, pp. 115–27

Miller, R. and Whitehead, C. (2015) *Inside Out and Upside Down: Community Based Approaches to Social Care Prevention in a Time of Austerity*, Birmingham: University of Birmingham

Miller, T. and Hall, G. (2013) *Letting Go: Breathing New Life into Organisations*, Argyll: Argyll Publishing

Morgan, A. (2014) 'Revisiting the asset model: A clarification of terms and ideas', *Global Health Promotion*, Vol. 21, pp. 3–6

Morgan, A. and Ziglio, E. (2007) 'Revitalising the evidence base for public health: An assets model', IUHPE – Promotion & Education Supplement 2, *Global Health Promotion*, Vol. 14, No. 2, pp. 17–22; doi: 10.1177/10253823070140020701x

Morgan, S. (2014) *Working with Strengths: Putting Personalisation and Recovery into Practice*, East Sussex: Pavilion Publishing

Morton, S. and Wright, A. (2015) 'Getting evidence into action to improve Scotland's public services' (online). Available from URL: http://whatworksscotland.ac.uk/wp-content/uploads/2015/02/WWS-Morton-Wright-Working-paper.pdf (accessed 11 January 2016)

Munro, E. (2004) *The Impact of Audit on Social Work Practice*, London: London School of Economics

Munro, E. (2010) 'The Munro review of child protection, part one: A systems analysis' (online). Available from URL: www.gov.uk/government/publications/munro-review-of-child-protection-part-1-a-systems-analysis (accessed 15 February 2016)

Munro, F (2015) *IRISS On … Place Based Working*, Glasgow: Institute for Research and Innovation in Social Services

Nesta (2012) *Working for Co-Production in Healthcare: Insights from Practitioners*, London: Nesta

Newlin, M., Webber, M., Morris, D. and Howarth, S. (2015) 'Social Participation Interventions for adults with mental health problems: a review and narrative synthesis', *Social Work Research*, Vol. 39, No. 3, pp. 167–80

NICE (2014) *Guidance: Behaviour Change: Individual Approaches*, London: NICE

Nicolay, C. R., Purkayastha, S., Greenhalgh, A., Benn, J., Chaturvedi, S., Phillips, N. and Darzi, A. (2011) 'Systematic review of the application of quality improvement methodologies from the manufacturing industry to surgical healthcare', *British Journal of Surgery*, Vol. 99, No. 3, pp. 324–35

Noble, K. G., Houston, S. M., Brito, N. H., Bartsch, H., Kan, E., Kuperman, J. M., Akshoomoff, N., Amaral, D. G., Bloss, C. S., Libiger, O., Schork, N. J., Murray, S. S., Casey, B. J., Chang, L., Ernst, T. M., Frazier, J. A., Gruen, J. R., Kennedy, D. N., Van Zijl, P., Mostofsky, S., Kaufmann, W. E., Kenet, T., Dale, A. M., Jernigan, T. L. and Sowell, E. R. (2015) 'Family income, parental education and brain structure in children and adolescents', *Nature Neuroscience*, Vol. 18, pp. 773–8

Novell, R. J. (2014) 'I want to fight for social work but I will not fight for bureaucracy', *The Guardian*. Available from URL: www.theguardian.com/social-care-network/social-life-blog/2014/dec/10/social-work-bureaucracy-paperwork-stifling (accessed 31 July 2015)

Nussbaum, M. C. (2011) *Creating Capabilities: the human development approach*, Cambridge, MA: Harvard University Press

Nutley, S., Powell, A. and Davies, H. (2013) *What Counts as Good Evidence?*, St Andrews: University of St Andrews, Alliance for Useful Evidence

O'Leary, T., Burkett, I. and Braithwaite, K. (2011) *Appreciating Assets*, Dunfermline: Carnegie UK Trust and International Association for Community Development

ODS Consulting (2014) *Evaluation of the Link Up Programme*, Edinburgh: Inspiring Scotland

OECD (2011) *How's Life?: Measuring Well-Being*, Paris: OECD Publishing

Ogilvie, D., Mitchell, R., Mutrie, N., Petticrew, M. and Platt, S. (2006) 'Evaluating the health effects of transport interventions: methodological case study', *American Journal of Preventative Medicine*, Vol. 31, pp. 118–26

Oxfam Scotland (2012) 'The Oxfam Humankind Index for Scotland. The new measure of Scotland's prosperity' (online), Oxfam Research Paper. Available from URL: http://policy-practice.oxfam.org.uk/our-work/poverty-in-the-uk/humankind-index (accessed 11 January 2016)

Park, N. and Peterson, C. (2006) 'Moral competence and character strengths among adolescents: The development and validation of the values in action inventory of strengths for youth', *Journal of Adolescence*, Vol. 29, pp. 891–910

Parrado, S., Van Ryzin, G. G., Bovaird, T. and Löeffler, E. (2013) 'Correlates of co-production: Evidence from a five-nation survey of citizens', *International Public Management Journal*, Vol. 16, No. 1, pp. 85–112

Pattoni, L. (2012) *Strengths-Based Approaches for Working with Individuals*, Insight 16, Glasgow: Institute for Research and Innovation in Social Services

Payne, N. (2001) 'Occupational stressors and coping as determinants of burnout in female hospice nurses', *Journal of Advanced Nursing*, Vol. 33, No. 3, pp. 396–405

Pearce, J. (2008) *'We Make Progress Because We Are Lost': Critical Reflections on Co Producing Knowledge as a Methodology for Researching Non Governmental Public Action*, London: London School of Economic

Penna, S., Paylor, I. and Soothill, K. (1995) *Job Satisfaction and Dissatisfaction Amongst Residential Care Workers*, York: Joseph Rowntree Foundation

Pestoff, V., Brandsen, T. and Verschuere, B. (2012) *New Public Governance, the Third Sector, and Co-Production*, Routledge Critical Studies in Public Management, New York: Routledge

Petch, A. (2013) *Delivering Integrated Care and Support*, Glasgow: Institute for Research and Innovation in Social Services

Petts, J., Horlick-Jones, T. and Murdock, G. (2001) *Social Amplification of Risk: The Media and the Public*, Sudbury: HSE Books

Popple, K. (1995) *Analysing Community Work: Its Theory and Practice*, Buckingham: Open University Press

Post, S. (2005) 'Altruism, happiness and health: It's good to good', *International Journal of Behavioural Health*, Vol. 12, pp. 66–77

Pratt, R., MacGregor, A., Reid, S. and Given, L. (2013) 'Experience of wellness recovery action planning in mutual support groups for people with lived experience of mental health difficulties', *The Scientific World Journal*; doi:10.1155/2013/180587

Propper, C. and Wilson, D. (2003) 'The Use and Usefulness of Performance Measures in the Public Sector', CMPO Working Paper Series No. 03/073, *Oxford Review of Economic Policy*, Vol. 19, No. 2, pp. 250–67

Pulla, V. (2012) 'What are strengths based practices all about?', in Pulla, V, Chenoweth, L., Francis, A. and Bakaj, S. (eds) (2012) *Papers in Strengths Based Practice*, New Delhi: Allied Publishers

Qureshi, H. (2001) *Outcomes in social care practice*, York: University of York, Social Policy Research Unit

Rapp, R. C., Siegal, H. A., Li, L. and Saha, P. (1998) 'Predicting post-primary treatment services and drug use outcome: A multivariate analysis', *American Journal of Drug and Alcohol Abuse*, Vol. 24, pp. 603–15

RCN (2014) *The Buurtzorg Nederland (Home Care Provider) Model, Observations from the United Kingdom*, London: Royal College of Nursing

Resolution Foundation (2015) 'Making the most of UC: Final report of the Resolution Foundation review of Universal Credit' (online). Available from URL: www.resolutionfoundation.org/publications/making-it-work-final-report-of-the-resolution-foundation-review-of-universal-credit (accessed 31 July 2015)

Richardson, L. (2011) *Working in Neighbourhoods in Bradford: An Interim Summary of Findings from the JRF Bradford Programme*, York: Joseph Rowntree Foundation

Rotegard, A. K., Moore, S. M., Fagermoen, M. S. and Ruland, C. M. (2010) 'Health assets: A concept analysis', *International Journal of Nursing Studies*, Vol. 47, pp. 513–25

Russell, C. (2004) 'Only connect: commissioning from an asset-based perspective' (online). Available from URL: http://blog.nurturedevelopment. org/2014/09/16/only-connect-commissioning-from-an-asset-based-perspective (accessed 31 August 2015)

Rustin, M. (2010) 'From the beginning to the end of Neo-Liberalism in Britain' (online). Available from URL: https://www.opendemocracy.net/ourkingdom/mike-rustin/after-neo-liberalism-in-britain (accessed 31 October 2015)

Saint-Jacques, M., Turcotte, D. and Pouliot, E. (2009) 'Adopting a strengths perspective in social work practice with families in difficulty: From theory to practice', *Families in Society: The Journal of Contemporary Social Services*, Vol. 90, No. 4, pp. 454–61

Saleebey, D. (2006) *The Strengths Perspective in Social Work Practice* (4th edn), Boston: Pearson Education

Savage, V., O'Sullivan, C., Mulgan, C. and Ali, R. (2009) *Public Services and Civil Society Working Together. An Initial Think Piece*, London: The Young Foundation

SCDC (2003) *LEAP for Health: Learning, Evaluation and Planning*, Edinburgh: NHS Health Scotland

SCDC (2011) *Community Development and Co-Production: Issues for Policy and Practice*, SCDC Discussion Paper 2011/02, Glasgow: Scottish Community Development Centre

SCDC (2012) *Building Stronger Communities*, Glasgow: Scottish Community Development Centre

SCDC (2014) *Towards Empowerment? Briefing on the Community Empowerment (Scotland) Bill and Call for Evidence*, Glasgow: Scottish Community Development Centre

SCDC (n.d.) 'Community-led health' (online). Available from URL: www.scdc.org.uk/community-led-health (accessed 31 July 2015)

SCIE (2010) *Enabling Risk, Ensuring Safety: Self-Directed Support and Personal Budgets*, London: Social Care Institute for Excellence

SCIE (2013) *Co-Production in Social Care: What It Is and How To Do It*, London: Social Care Institute for Excellence. Available from URL: www.scie.org.uk/publications/guides/guide51 (accessed 31 May 2015)

ScotPHO (2010) 'ScotPHO Online Profiles Tool (OPT)' (online). Available from URL: www.scotpho.org.uk/comparative-health/profiles/online-profiles-tool (accessed 31 August 2015)

Scottish Executive (1997) *Designed to Care – Renewing the NHS in Scotland*, Edinburgh: Scottish Executive

Scottish Executive (1999) *Towards a Healthier Scotland*, Edinburgh: Scottish Executive

Scottish Executive (2003) *Improving Health in Scotland: The Challenge*, Edinburgh: Scottish Executive

Scottish Executive (2005a) *Building a Health Service Fit for the Future. A Report on the Future of the NHS in Scotland. (Kerr Report)*, Edinburgh: Scottish Government and NHS Scotland

Scottish Executive (2005b) *Delivering for Health*, Edinburgh: Scottish Executive and NHS Scotland

Scottish Government (2006) *Changing Lives: Report of the twenty-first century Social Work Review*, Edinburgh: Scottish Government

Scottish Government (2007) *Better Health, Better Care*, Edinburgh: Scottish Government and NHS Scotland

Scottish Government (2008) *The Early Years Framework*, Edinburgh: Scottish Government

Scottish Government (2010a) *Annual Report of the Chief Medical Officer. Health in Scotland 2009 Time for Change*, Edinburgh: NHS Scotland and Scottish Government

Scottish Government (2010b) *The Healthcare Quality Strategy for NHS Scotland*, Edinburgh: Scottish Government

Scottish Government (2011a) *Annual Report of the Chief Medical Officer. Health in Scotland 2010 Assets for All*, Edinburgh: NHS Scotland and Scottish Government

Scottish Government (2011b) *Achieving Sustainable Quality in Scotland's Healthcare: A 20:20 Vision*, Edinburgh: Scottish Government and NHS Scotland

Scottish Government (2011c) *Renewing Scotland's Public Services. Priorities for Reform in Response to The Christie Commission*, Edinburgh: Scottish Government

Scottish Government (2011d) *Achieving a Sustainable Future Scotland's Regeneration Strategy*, Edinburgh: Scottish Government

Scottish Government (2013) *Everyone Matters: 2020 Workforce Vision*, Edinburgh: Scottish Government and NHS Scotland

Scottish Government (2014) *The Public Bodies (Joint Working) (National Health and Wellbeing Outcomes) (Scotland) Regulations 2014*, Edinburgh: Scottish Government

Scottish Government (2015) *Social Services in Scotland: A Shared Vision and Strategy*, Edinburgh: Scottish Government

Scottish Government (n.d.a) 'Public health review' (online). Available from URL: www.gov.scot/Topics/Health/Healthy-Living/Public-Health-Review (accessed 31 July 2015)

Scottish Government (n.d.b) 'Scotland performs' (online). Available from URL: www.gov.scot/About/Performance/scotPerforms (accessed October 2015)

Scottish Parliament (1968) 'Social Work (Scotland) Act 1968' (online). Available from URL: www.legislation.gov.uk/ukpga/1968/49/contents (accessed 30 September 2015)

Scottish Parliament (2013a) 'Social Care (Self Directed Support) Act 2013' (online). Available from URL: www.legislation.gov.uk/asp/2013/1/contents/enacted (accessed 30 September 2015)

Scottish Parliament (2013b) 'The Requirements for Community Learning and Development (Scotland) Regulations 2013' (online). Available from URL: www.legislation.gov.uk/ssi/2013/175/pdfs/ssi_20130175_en.pdf (accessed 30 September 2015)

Scottish Parliament (2013c) 'Public Bodies (Joint Working) (Scotland) Bill' (online). Available from URL: www.scottish.parliament.uk/help/63845.aspx (accessed 31 July 2015)

Scottish Parliament (2015a) 'Community Empowerment (Scotland) Act

2015' (online). Available from URL: www.legislation.gov.uk/asp/2015/6/
contents/enacted (accessed 30 September 2015)

Scottish Parliament (2015b) 'Land Reform (Scotland) Bill' (online). Available
from http://www.scottish.parliament.uk/S4_Bills/Land%20Reform%20
(Scotland)%20Bill/SPBill76BS042016.pdf (accessed 30 September 2015
and 30 March 2016)

Seddon, J. (2008) *Systems Thinking in the Public Sector: The Failure of the
Reform Regime … and a Manifesto for a Better Way*, Axminster: Triarchy
Press

Senge, P. (1990) *The Fifth Discipline: The Art and Practice of the Learning
Organization*, London: Century Business

Sharp, C. (2012) *When Are You Ever Not 'Piloting'? How Action Research Can
Help to Deliver Better Public Services*, Edinburgh: Research for Real

Shiell-Davis, K. (2015) *What Works Scotland: Scaling-Up innovations*, Edinburgh: What Works Scotland

Sigerson, D. and Gruer, L. (2011) *Asset-Based Approaches to Health Improvement, Evidence for Action*, Glasgow: NHS Health Scotland

Skeffington, A. (1969) *People and Planning: Report of the Committee in
Public Participation in Planning*. London: Ministry of Housing and Local
Government

Skinner, S. (2006) *Strengthening Communities*, London: Community Development Foundation

Slay, J. and Penny, J. (2014) *Commissioning for Outcomes and Co-Production.
Guidance for Local Authorities*, London: New Economics Foundation

Smith, M. and Herren, S. (2011) *More Than GDP: Measuring What Matters*,
Dunfermline: Carnegie UK Trust

Smock, S. A., Trepper, T. S., Wetchler, J. L., McCollum, E. E., Ray, R. and
Pierce, K. (2008) 'Solution-focused group therapy for level 1 substance
abusers', *Journal of Marital and Family Therapy*, Vol. 34, No. 1, pp. 107–20.
Available from URL: www.ncbi.nlm.nih.gov/pubmed/18199184 (accessed
15 February 2016)

South, J. (2015) *A Guide to Community-Centred Approach to Health and Well-
being*, London: Public Health England

South, J., White, J. and Gamsu, M. (2013) *People Centred Public Health*. Bristol:
The Policy Press

Staudt, M., Howard, M. O. and Drake, B. (2001) 'The operationalization,
implementation, and effectiveness of the strengths perspective: A review of
empirical studies', *Journal of Social Service Research*, Vol. 27, No. 3, pp. 1–21

Steptoe, A. and Feldman, P. J. (2001) 'Neighbourhood problems as a source
of chronic stress: Development of a measure of neighbourhood problems,
and associations with socioeconomic status and health', *Annuals of Behavioural Medicine*, Vol. 23, pp. 177–85

Stiglitz, J., Sen, A. and Fitoussi, J. P. (2009) 'Report by the Commission on
the measurement of economic performance and social progress' (online).
Available from URL: www.stiglitz-sen-fitoussi.fr/en/index.htm (accessed
31 May 2015)

Stocks-Rankin, C. R. (2015) *Pathways to Impact: IRISS Through the Lens of*

Contribution Analysis, Glasgow: Institute for Research and Innovation in Social Services

Taylor, M. (2003) *Public Policy in the Community*, 1st edn, London: Palgrave Macmillan

Thomas, B., Dorling, D, and Davey Smith, G. (2010) 'Inequalities in premature mortality in Britain: observational study from 1921 to 2007', *British Medical Journal*, 341: c3639; doi:10.1136/bmj.c3639

Tobi, P., Sheridan, K. and Findlay, G. (2014) 'Developing a systematic approach to asset based health and social needs assessment', *European Journal of Public Health*, 24 (Supplement 2); doi:10.1093/eurpub/cku166.014 cku166.014

Unwin, J. (2014) 'The voluntary sector needs to reclaim its identity and set its own course', in Slocock, C. (ed.) (2014) *Making Good Ess*ays, London: Civil Exchange. Available from URL: http://baringfoundation.org.uk/wp-content/uploads/2014/11/MakingGoodEssays.pdf (accessed 15 February 2016)

Van den Bergh, J. and Antal, M. (2014) *Evaluating Alternatives to GDP as Measures of Social Welfare/Progress*, Vienna: Welfare Wealth Work for Europe

Vanderplasschen, W., Wolf, J., Rapp, R. C. and Broekaert, E. (2007) 'Effectiveness of different models of case management for substance abusing populations', *Journal of Psychoactive Drugs*, Vol. 39, No. 1, pp. 81–95. Available from URL: www.ncbi.nlm.nih.gov/pmc/articles/PMC1986794 (accessed 15 February 2016)

Verschuere, B., Brandsen, T. and Pestoff, V. (2012) 'Co-production: The state of the art in research and the future agenda', *Voluntas*, Vol. 23, No. 4, pp. 1083–101

Voorberg, W. H., Bekkes, V. J. J. M. and Tummers, L. G. (2014) 'A systematic review of co-creation and co-production: Embarking on the social innovation journey', *Public Management Review*, Vol. 17, pp. 1333–57; doi: 10.1080/14719037.2014.930505

Wallace, J. (2013) *The Rise of the Enabling State: A Review of the Policy and Evidence across the UK and Ireland*, Dunfermline: Carnegie UK

Webel, A. R., Okonsky, J., Trompeta, J. and Holsemer, W. (2010) 'A systematic review of the effectiveness of peer-based interventions on health-related behaviors in adults', *American Journal of Public Health*, Vol. 100, No. 2, pp. 247–53

Weiss, C. H. (2001) 'Theory-based evaluation: Theories of change for poverty reduction programmes', in Feinstein, N, and Picciotto, R. (eds) (2001) *Evaluation and Poverty Reduction*, New Brunswick, NJ: Transaction

Welsh Assembly Government (2011) *Fairer Health Outcomes for All*, Cardiff: Welsh Assembly Government

West, M. A., Eckert, R., Steward, K. and Pasmore, B. (2014) *Developing Collective Leadership for Healthcare*, London: The King's Fund

WHO (1986) *Ottawa Charter for Health Promotion*, Venice: World Health Organization

WHO (n.d.) 'Human rights-based approach to health' (online). Available from URL: www.who.int/trade/glossary/story054/en (accessed 31 August 2015)

Wieringa, S. and Greenhalgh, T. (2015) '10 years of mindlines: A systematic review and commentary', *Implementation Science*, Vol. 10, p. 45

Wilkinson, R. and Picket, K. (2009) *The Spirit Level: Why More Equal Societies Almost Always Do Better*, London: Penguin

Wilson, J. (2000) 'Volunteering', *Annual Reviews of Sociology*, Vol. 26, pp. 215–40

Wimbush, E., Montague, S. and Mulherin, T. (2012) 'Applications of contribution analysis to outcome planning and evaluation', *Evaluation*, Vol. 18, No. 3, pp. 10–29

INDEX

Note: page numbers in *italics* denote tables or figures